BUSINESS **IS A**
CONTACT SPORT

BUSINESS **IS A** CONTACT SPORT

Using the 12 Principles of

Relationship Asset

Management to

Build Buy-In,

Blast Away Barriers, and

Boost Your Business

TOM RICHARDSON
AUGUSTO VIDAURRETA
WITH TOM GORMAN

A Pearson Education Company

International Standard Book Number: 0-02-864163-9
Library of Congress Catalog Card Number: 2001092307

04   03   02   8   7   6   5   4   3   2   1

Interpretation of the printing code: The rightmost number of the first series of numbers is the year of the book's printing; the rightmost number of the second series of numbers is the number of the book's printing. For example, a printing code of 02-1 shows that the first printing occurred in 2002.

Printed in the United States of America

To my hero,
William E. Richardson, my dad.
—Tom Richardson

To my lovely family—
my wife Jeanie, my daughters Kaitlyn and Alexis,
my mother Esther, my father Augusto, and my sister Esther Maria.
—Augusto Vidaurreta

TABLE OF CONTENTS

Introduction: A Whole New Ballgame iv

Principle #1   See Relationships as Valuable Assets 2

Principle #2   Develop a Game Plan 24

Principle #3   Create Ownership for Relationships 42

Principle #4   Transform Contacts into Connections 62

Principle #5   Move into the Win-Win Zone 80

Principle #6   Get to Know Your Stakeholders as People....................100

Principle #7   Build Bonds of Trust with All Stakeholders.................116

Principle #8   Banish Relationship Killers 132

Principle #9   When Something Breaks, Fix It Fast...........148

Principle #10   Get Rolling and Maintain Momentum........................168

Principle #11   Maximize the Long-Term Value of Relationships 188

Principle #12   Keep the Wins Coming, Stakeholder by Stakeholder 208

Epilogue: Uncommon Common Sense........................232

Appendix: Target Wins for Company-Stakeholder Relationships...234

Index 248

A WHOLE NEW BALLGAME

When we say business is a contact sport, we mean that making contact—and building relationships—is, and always will be, the path to success. We do not mean contact in terms of demolishing the opposition, as in football or boxing. We mean that establishing, building, and maintaining relationships in a well-planned, well-executed manner will enable you to excel in whatever you do.

We wrote this book because we took a different approach to business and it became the driver of our success. We understood the power of relationships, not only with employees and customers, as important as they are, but with everyone our business endeavors touched. With that understanding, we built our first company and all our subsequent businesses faster and more profitably than we had ever dreamed possible. The approach that we take and the things that we do are embodied in the principles in this book. Together, these principles constitute Relationship Asset Management, or RAM.

Until recently, when we sat in our offices and marveled at how RAM was helping us succeed, often one of us would say, "I wish there was a way we could package this and pass it along to others." This book is that package. RAM represents a formula—virtually a step-by-step plan—for success in business, or in any other field. But before we get more deeply into RAM, a bit about who we are is probably in order.

We are entrepreneurs and investors who, in 1988, left professional positions as consultants at Arthur Andersen and, with a $100 investment used to incorporate the company, started Systems Consulting Group. SCG was an information technology consulting firm focused on IT strategy and implementation. Over the next seven years, revenues skyrocketed. The company was profitable in every year and never needed a dime in outside capital. In an industry where employee turnover averaged 20 to 30 percent annually, ours ran between 4 and 5 percent. Moreover, we employed *no sales force.* New business came almost entirely from referrals from our suppliers, vendors, strategic partners, and other word-of-mouth sources. Our employees were so committed to the company's success that each of them became a one-man or one-woman sales force.

Using the principles you'll learn in this book, we attracted and retained blue-chip clients such as M&M Mars, Quaker Oats, NYNEX, Bell Atlantic, Federal Express, Blockbuster Entertainment, GE Capital, Ryder System, W.R. Grace, Campbell's Soup, Pillsbury, and Burger King. In 1992 and 1994, SCG made Inc. magazine's list of the 500 fastest-growing companies in the United States. In 1996, we were named Entrepreneur of the Year finalists in Florida. Although we didn't start the company with the goal of cashing out, our rapid growth and first-rate client roster made us an attractive acquisition target to a number of larger consulting firms. In 1995, Cambridge Technology Partners made us an offer we couldn't refuse and acquired SCG for $30 million in a stock-swap transaction. (This occurred before the late-1990s Internet and tech-stock valuation craze.)

Since then, we've founded Horizon Bank in South Florida; established Hardaway's Firehouse Four, a full-service restaurant in downtown Miami; started Entente, a venture capital firm, and Adjoined Technologies, a consulting firm; and become involved in various roles in the hotel and resort business (the Canopy Palms in Singer Island and the Radisson Riverwalk in Jacksonville, Florida) and in P&O Packaging, a plastics manufacturer.

We mention all this because we attribute our success completely to Relationship Asset Management. We didn't discover RAM, we developed it. In the beginning it was an expression of our values—honesty, trust, fairness, teamwork, doing unto others as we would have them do unto us, and a bit of "You only go around once, so you may as well enjoy yourself." Eventually, this became a way of doing business. And it works.

We've proven it to ourselves. Moreover, business schools around the country are agreeing. Future business curriculums will have a RAM component to them, and we expect that most corporate strategies will as well.

Here's why: The current business environment tends to work against relationships. Companies merge with one another in alarming numbers. New competitors pop up out of nowhere. People change jobs—employers, not positions within an employer—an average of every three years. After more than a decade of reengineering, many large companies are still downsizing. Developments in technology, particularly information technology, redefine boundaries, businesses, and entire industries every 12 months. At least.

In addition:

- Customers are tougher than ever, seeking the best deal on every transaction, with "best" defined—at that moment—by price, quality, service, warranty, or compatibility.
- Employees with short-term horizons demand full payment for their contributions, along with satisfying job content, professional status, and control over their work lives.
- Suppliers can be acquired overnight by someone you don't know or strike a deal with a competitor that can threaten your sources of raw material or product.
- Investors, both institutional and individual, will readily sell their stake in a company for a higher return elsewhere.
- Boards of directors, once sleepy clubs, have been shaken awake by new legal exposures and the shareholder rights movement.
- Communities that once welcomed business as a source of jobs and tax revenue also contain activists with often overwhelming environmental and social agendas.

Relationships with these and other parties, such as the media, charities, and government agencies, have become more complex, more tumultuous, and more important than ever.

Why more important? Three reasons stand out:

First, the communications revolution and the age of the Internet have insured that everyone is connected to everyone else. This affects a company for better or worse, depending on how you treat people. Good relationships beget good relationships, poor relationships beget bad ones. Actions reverberate and word travels fast. That can be good or bad for an organization, depending upon the word that's getting around.

Second, many people play multiple roles vis-à-vis an organization. They may be customers or employees *and* investors *and* community members *and* supporters of a charity. People want to be treated well regardless of the position they're playing.

Third, and most important, a company can gain tremendous competitive advantage by successfully managing its relationships. You not only avoid problems—employee turnover, customer attrition, supply disruptions, expensive lawsuits, and malicious gossip—but also gain financially (we'll show you how) and build a storehouse of goodwill. The result? Competent employees, long-term customers, cooperative suppliers, committed investors, sympathetic media—a supportive team of people with a stake in your company's success.

We call our system Relationship Asset Management because relationships are valuable business *assets*. As such, they need to be actively managed. On one level, the principles in this book are simple. They involve understanding who can help you reach your business goals, building connections with those people, crafting mutually beneficial deals, avoiding problems, fixing those that do arise, and, ultimately, building a network of long-term, trusting, win-win relationships.

RAM is a business strategy. This is not about being nice for the sake of being nice. It's about managing what we see as the single most valuable asset a company or person possesses. Relationships represent a unique strategic resource that cannot be appropriated, duplicated, or stolen, all of which can happen to a product, process, or technology. Thus, relationships are not only assets, they are irreplaceable assets.

RAM aims to consistently create mutual wins for all stakeholders in a relationship. We believe that maximizing mutual wins, and only maximizing mutual wins benefits, will maximize the value of a relationship to both parties. And nothing is more valuable than a valuable relationship.

THE WINS FOR YOU IN THIS BOOK

In this book, we've broken RAM down into 12 principles. We view these principles as the fundamentals that ensure success in business. As a matter of fact, although we write from the perspective of our business backgrounds, these principles ensure success in any endeavor. These are also principles of successful living, not just from the financial standpoint—although that's important—but from the standpoint of your social and family life.

Every—and we do mean every—business can benefit from an asset management approach to its relationships. Our experience, and that of hundreds of other businesses, shows that our approach enables a company to …

- Attract, retain, and motivate valuable employees.
- Boost the effectiveness of sales, marketing, dealer, and distribution efforts.
- Bolster investor confidence and improve access to funding.
- Strengthen community relations and attract positive media coverage.
- Broaden and improve the range of available business opportunities.
- Strengthen the company, lengthen its life, and dramatically improve its long-term financial performance.

The principles of RAM will also benefit you as a professional and as a person. If you are an entrepreneur, business owner, corporate executive, manager, employee at any level, investor, student, or volunteer, RAM will show you how to …

- Form alliances with people who can help you and whom you can help.
- Access the ideas, talents, and knowledge of a much wider range of people than would otherwise be available to you.
- Reduce daily on-the-job tension, frustration, and disappointment through increased goodwill among your co-workers and associates.
- Increase your value to your company and—we are willing to bet—to the world, by taking a positive, proactive, win-centric approach to everyone you deal with in your business.

You can apply our system—no, you *must* apply our system—not just to customers and employees but to everyone your business touches, because in our system everybody counts. That means that you can learn, practice, and master these principles no matter what business you're in, no matter what position you play, and no matter where you are in your career. When you approach business as a "contact sport" you will succeed, and help others succeed, in ways that you have certainly dreamed about but probably have never achieved in the past.

If we succeed in promulgating the principles of RAM, changes will take place in the way businesses think about and manage their relationships. We believe that someday when equity and acquisition analysts examine a company, they will first ask, "Tell us about your relationship with each of your stakeholders." Relationships will be recognized as the assets that they are, and those analysts will weigh their value in valuations of the company. When that happens, where will your business be? What will be the value of your relationship assets?

In the Darwinian world of business, where natural selection rules as it does in nature, Relationship Asset Management is quite simply the next giant evolutionary step.

Here's to a whole new ballgame.

ACKNOWLEDGMENTS

This book originated in the experiences we had building relationships over the years with our friends, associates, colleagues, and stakeholders of every type. We especially extend our thanks to our employees, clients, suppliers, vendors, bankers, and the nonprofit organizations we worked with while we established and grew Systems Consulting Group (SCG) and our other ventures. Our heartfelt appreciation goes to all of you, expecially Jeff Manchester, Sandy Strauss, and Bill Dudziak, our partners at SCG. Thanks also to all of our friends and co-workers at SCG Adjoined Technologies, P&O Packaging, Horizon Bank, Canopy Palms Resort, The Jacksonville Radisson Riverwalk, and Hardaway's Firehouse Four.

The process of writing this book involved several presentations and interactions with students and faculty. We especially acknowledge the contributions of professors and students at Carnegie Mellon University, University of Miami, University of Florida, Florida International University, University of Maryland, and University of Arizona. They challenged a number of concepts and improved the book markedly.

Several friends also contributed their ideas and constructive criticism along the way, including Dr. Lew Temares, Dean of Engineering at the University of Miami; Dr. Joyce Elam, Dean of the College of Business at Florida International University; and Father Francis ("Skip") Flynn, whom we also thank for keeping our heads steady throughout the process.

The publishing professionals on this project literally made the book happen. Special thanks go to our collaborator Tom Gorman for finding the words and building the manuscript. Thanks also to Harvey Ardman for his work on earlier drafts. Our agent, Mike Snell, and our energetic editor, Renee Wilmeth, guided us through the publishing process. We thank them and the entire team at Alpha Books, including senior production editor Christy Wagner, copy editor Krista Hansing, and production members Angela Calvert and John Etchison. We would also like to thank our publicist, Jodee Blanco, for her efforts in promoting the book.

We also thank our families, friends, co-workers, and stakeholders-at-large for their loyalty, support, and interest and for helping us jointly craft Relationship Asset Management and demonstrate its power. To all of you we raise a glass and say, *"Salud!"*

Tom Richardson
Augusto Vidaurreta
Miami, Florida

SEE RELATIONSHIPS AS VALUABLE ASSETS

I cannot stress too often that a quarterback is not in the game by himself, nor should he expect to bear all the burdens of conducting the offense. Successful quarterbacks want as much solid and useful information as they can get during a game, and one who tries to do it all on his own is heading for some disappointing game days.

—*From* The Art of Quarterbacking, *by Ken Anderson of the Cincinnati Bengals*

Professional athletes are never in the game by themselves, and they always want as much useful information as they can get. The quarterback might be seen as the star of the team, but in his book, Ken Anderson goes on to say that besides listening to the coach, the QB needs to tune in to the guys in the backfield, the linemen, and even the players on the sidelines. To win the game, he needs every one of these people—not just for their blocking, tackling, running, and receiving, but also for their perspectives on threats and opportunities unfolding on the field and how to deal with them.

Savvy managers, entrepreneurs, and professionals understand that they, too, are surrounded by people who can help them. They see their relationships with those people as valuable assets, and that is the first principle of Relationship Asset Management (RAM). When you see relationships as assets, you focus on them. You are attuned to every one of them, and you employ them to move your organization and everyone with a stake in it toward their goals. You realize that without relationships, you don't have a business. And you know that when you're on top of your business relationships, you're on top of your game.

MINING THE VALUE IN RELATIONSHIPS

We're here to blow the whistle and call a timeout! We want you to join us in a huddle and hear a game-winning idea: You've got to protect your assets out there—and put them to work for you and your company.

Is this warning necessary? Aren't managers and entrepreneurs already managing their assets? Aren't they tracking down materials breakage and plugging inventory leaks? Don't they immediately put idle equipment and empty office space to use? Aren't they ridding the shop floor of wasted time and motion? Haven't they declared open season on fraud, embezzlement, uncollected debts, and other financial losses?

Of course. Yet they often sit stone still as some of their most valuable assets leak out, sit idle, or lose money. The assets in question are the company's current and potential relationships. So, we're saying, let's take a look at what's happening to our business relationships and develop a game plan for identifying, evaluating, developing, and protecting these assets.

The fact is, many managers don't see their relationships as assets. True, most know that customer relationships are important. The same goes for those with employees. However, as important as those two stakeholder groups are, they are just part of the picture. Every relationship that the company has with everyone it touches—or could benefit from touching—is an asset or a potential asset. In business, assets must be mined for their full value. That's the approach to their relationships that we recommend managers and entrepreneurs take.

Many companies don't fully consider the role that relationships play in their business. For instance, in the early to mid-1990s, a major cereal, cookie, and snack food company laid off a large portion of its veteran sales force. These men and women were being paid more than the company would have to pay younger, less experienced recruits. So, in a typical economically driven personnel decision, management laid off large numbers of seasoned salespeople. The move was justified by financial strategy, which aimed to cut costs—a common objective for companies in mature markets. The move also seemed justified by marketing strategy. After all, with long-established, household-name brands, management believed that the products had a permanent franchise on supermarket shelf space. Didn't they basically sell themselves?

Not exactly. From 1996 through 1999, the company's total annual cookie, snack, and cereal sales decreased dramatically. Analysts reported that the company had underestimated how important the relationships that its salespeople had formed with supermarket and grocery-store managers were. It turned out that the battle for shelf space depends on more than having solid brands. It also depends on the relationships that a company's salespeople have with the people who control the shelf space in the stores.

The relationships that those salespeople had built with the store managers over the years were valuable assets. Those assets were destroyed in a matter of weeks because of one management decision. Implicit in that decision was the failure to view relationships—in this case, relationships between salespeople and customers—as assets.

Assets enable a company to reach its goals. That's why assets have value and why companies invest in them, manage them, and maximize the use of them. That's also why relationships are assets: They enable a company to reach its goals. We're convinced that a major reason so many companies don't manage their relationships as assets is that managers don't fully understand the role that relationships play in reaching goals. Or maybe relationships are too intangible for most managers to see as assets. Yet information is intangible, and most companies now view it as being on par with the traditional resources of land, labor, and capital. The investment of billions of dollars in information technology and the creation of the position of chief information officer both attest to that. However, a company needs relationships with employees, customers, suppliers, investors, government agencies, competitors, and a huge array of other entities and individuals as surely as it needs offices, computers, vehicles, and information.

No business of any size can function without relationships because they provide the context in which people do business. When that context is missing—when people don't really know one another, or when relationships are distorted by mistrust, greed, or bad feelings—doing business becomes far more difficult, if not impossible. The better a company's relationships are, the better that company will function. What's more, doing business by developing relationships is much easier, far more personally rewarding, and a lot more fun.

Microsoft might be the best recent example of a major company failing to manage all of its relationships effectively. As of this writing, Microsoft faces the possibility of a federally ordered break-up of the company. Whatever your opinion is of the court's decision (we have our opinion, too), and whatever the ultimate outcome of the case and the appeals to follow, one thing is certain: Microsoft did a poor job of managing its relationships with two important constituencies—its competitors and the government. As reported in the November 1, 1999, *New York Times,* complaints from Netscape Communications about Microsoft's competitive practices "captured the Justice Department's attention and touched off the investigation and trial." Two years before the trial, Sen. Orrin Hatch called Microsoft chairman Bill Gates before his judiciary committee and gave him "a political shellacking." Novell Corporation, another Microsoft competitor, is based in Utah, which happens to be Sen. Hatch's state.

With an 80 to 90 percent share of the world's microcomputer operating system market, these were risks that Microsoft could have foreseen. A near-monopoly actually benefits from competition—or, at least, the appearance of competition. For instance, in the commercial credit-reporting business, where Dun & Bradstreet has long held about an 85 percent share, D&B tolerates competitors, such as TRW's business credit-reporting division and other, smaller credit bureaus. With antitrust laws on the books, healthy competitors are arguably a key success factor for a near-monopoly. However, Microsoft's practices angered its few genuine competitors, who took their case to the government.

When Microsoft finally perceived the risks it faced, it began a serious lobbying and public relations effort. But that effort was occasionally clumsy and certainly too late. The *Times* article mentioned, "Mr. Gates long disdained the capitol [Washington, D.C.] as an analog anachronism in a digital age and refused to devote time or resources to courting government leaders. That has now changed, in a big way."

If a Relationship Asset Management strategy had been in place and had been properly executed, Netscape, Sun Microsystems, and Oracle would not have felt the need to counter Microsoft's market power with lobbying and campaign contributions. The government would not have received complaints—or, if it had, it might have taken measures short of literally making a federal case out of it. Yet, in all fairness, it would have taken extraordinary foresight for Microsoft to view a good relationship with the government as an asset. Few companies in unregulated industries do. Also, most companies automatically adopt an aggressive posture toward competitors. That's part of why our approach to relationship management is a whole new game. It views *all* relationships as assets, even those with the government and competitors.

The *Times* quoted a Washington attorney hired by Microsoft in 1998 as saying, "The company made a mistake years ago by not cultivating friends in government, academia, and the media. It's hard to do when you're in the middle of a problem. I've told them they have to *make friends before you need them, rather than after.*" We've italicized that last statement because it could serve as the mantra for all who would practice RAM.

FROM THE RAM PLAYBOOK

The notion that relationships with competitors can be assets strikes some managers as fanciful. But the speed of change in business means that most companies cannot "do it all" on their own. Even those that *can* do it all can't do it quickly enough or profitably enough if they go it alone. At Entente, our venture-capital/mentor-capital firm focused on the Internet consulting business, we found that when two companies actually analyze the regions, markets, and technologies where they compete, this usually amounts to 20 to 30 percent of their respective total operations. This is particularly true of small to medium-size companies. Considering the benefits that can accrue from cooperation, there's little sense in letting the 70 to 80 percent that holds potential be canceled out by the relatively small area of competition. Start talking with competitors. Try to see where you really compete and where you might be able to profit together. If at a minimum you only agree not to steal each other's employees, then you have won.

A company as mighty as Microsoft can be brought into a damaging action at law by its failure to develop relationships with its competitors and the government (despite its considerable skill at forging bonds with customers and employees). A well-established international snack and cereal company—with a first-rate merchandising operation—can lose millions of dollars in sales because it misjudged the value of relationships between salespeople and store managers. If that's the case at these leading companies, perhaps a "timeout" is in order so that we can all take stock of our relationship assets.

This process begins with an understanding of the Relationship Web.

THE RELATIONSHIP WEB

Consider what happens when a business fails. A whole universe of people feels the impact. Employees lose their jobs, sometimes their homes, and even sometimes their health and marriages. Suppliers undergo lay-offs, extending the misery further. Lenders are not repaid, and shareholders lose their investments. Charities and community groups lose funding and perhaps volunteers. A business failure reduces the state's sales tax revenue and property, payroll, and income tax collections. If a string of businesses fails or a large enough outfit goes under, the community will need to reduce public services, extending the effects to everyone in the vicinity.

Conversely, when a business flourishes and expands, a large number of people see their lives improve. Therefore, when we talk about relationships, we mean the relationships that the organization has with every entity or individual that it touches in any way. As noted, these relationships extend well beyond those with employees and customers. They include those within the organization, plus relationships with all those entities and individuals that form what we call the Relationship Web.

Every enterprise, large or small, profit or nonprofit, public or private, stands at the center of a web of relationships. (Similarly, each one of us stands at the center of our own personal Relationship Web.) Various strands connect the organization at the center to every entity and individual that it touches. It's best to think of those entities and individuals as stakeholders, as people with a stake in the success of the organization. For most publicly held (or to-be publicly held) companies, the key stakeholder groups could include these:

The Stakeholders:

- Employees
- Executives
- Customers
- Prospects
- Suppliers and vendors
- Accountants, attorneys, and other professional service providers
- Banks and other financial institutions
- Distributors and other resellers
- Strategic partners and alliances
- Licensors and licensees
- Complementors and competitors
- The board of directors
- Investors
- The investment community
- Security analysts
- The media
- Industry associations
- The community and the public
- Government officials, legislative bodies, and regulatory agencies
- Educational institutions

These stakeholder groups contain both entities and individuals, and when you think of your stakeholders, you need to consider both. In other words, your organization (an entity) and you (an individual) have relationships with entities (companies, nonprofit organizations, government agencies, and so on) and with the people within those entities. A relationship between two organizations consists of the various relationships among the people in those organizations. RAM is a way of managing relationships at all of these levels: entity to entity, entity to individual, and individual to individual.

Note that *former* members of these stakeholder groups might have a place in the outfit's Relationship Web. Smart companies try to part on good terms with employees, customers, investors, and partners who move on. It only makes sense. Although some companies will not rehire former employees, many do, and even those that don't can use good word of mouth. Also, customers often return when they find the grass no greener elsewhere. Investors come and go and come back, and a former distributor or partner might return for the right deal.

There might be a place in the Relationship Web for noncompetitors in the same industry. For example, a building contractor in Ohio has a lot in common with one in New Jersey. Large companies might compete in a specific service or region and not in others. To the extent that companies resemble one another, they should consider themselves reciprocal members of one another's Relationship Webs. Also, companies in unrelated businesses in the same region usually share interests in environmental and other regulation, labor and real-estate markets, and communication and transportation infrastructures. Good relationships benefit all parties affected by such issues.

True complementors, such as Intel and most PC manufacturers, or tire manufacturers and car companies, are naturally in each other's Relationship Webs. They belong there because they can help one another attain goals, enhance success factors, and mitigate risks. For example, if Intel designs into a chip certain functions performed by software, that action could reverberate for better or worse throughout its

Relationship Web. In such cases, it might be best for Intel to take a RAM approach and warn those companies so that they can prepare for the changes ahead.

A Relationship Web.

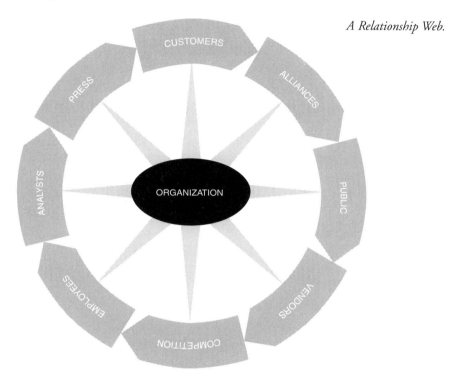

The virtual community—defined by the Internet—cannot be ignored because it now includes all stakeholders. The sheer size, growth, breadth, and speed of the World Wide Web mean that even companies without the dot-com suffix must consider it a constituency as well as a medium.

An organization's size, industry, structure, and other characteristics can indicate inclusion of other stakeholders not discussed here. Again, the more complete the inventory of stakeholders is at this point, the more accurate the picture of the Relationship Web.

FROM THE RAM PLAYBOOK

One of the most common mistakes in managing business relationships is prioritizing one stakeholder over another without fully considering the effects on other stakeholders. For instance, many management teams place the short-term needs of investors (or Wall Street) before those of all other stakeholders. This encourages decisions that boost the short-term stock price, often at the expense of the longer-term needs of employees, customers, or suppliers, which ultimately jeopardizes the longer-term interests of investors.

RAM aims for balanced growth in relationship assets and entails balancing the needs of the various stakeholders in the Relationship Web. Stakeholders' needs will shift from time to time as business, competitive, and organizational conditions change. When that happens, management's emphasis on meeting their needs will shift as well. Sometimes the needs of investors will come first. At other times, the needs of employees or customers or the community will take priority.

This doesn't mean that everyone necessarily gets a turn to be first or that all stakeholders have an equal stake in the company. It means that all stakeholders have a stake in the company's success and that however large or small that stake is, management must recognize and protect it. In making any decision, it's best to consider the potential impact on all stakeholders and to be certain to balance the stakeholders' wins over time.

As we examine the principles of RAM, we will refer to the Relationship Web from time to time. Not only does it depict some of the stakeholders that a company will have, it also illustrates that connections exist among them. This implies that a strategy of getting one stakeholder to recommend, work with, or otherwise be of value to another one can often be an effective relationship management tactic.

Several other points about the Relationship Web are worth noting:

- In day-to-day practice, strong business relationships are the result of solid personal relationships. Because relationships are personal, management must ensure that people at various levels take responsibility for their Relationship Webs and form relationships at various levels among stakeholders. Otherwise, an asset could be lost when someone leaves the organization.

- Like the snowflakes they resemble, no two Relationship Webs are exactly alike. Company size, location, purpose, culture, finances, capabilities, vision, language, legal structure, and other factors, even luck, dictate that every organization will have its own unique Relationship Web.

- A Relationship Web changes as entities within stakeholder groups merge, acquire one another, or go out of business and as individuals working in these entities resign or are transferred, promoted, or laid off. A supplier might be acquired by another company. A new product might attract new customers. A new director of a regulatory agency could take a more aggressive approach. The Relationship Web that an organization had a year ago, or even a week ago, might not be the one that it has today.

These points imply that RAM must occur on a personal basis and that it never ceases. Because it is personal, it cannot be left to "the organization." Instead, people within the organization must proactively establish and build relationships. There's no steady state because webs are in constant flux. A Relationship Web left to itself will drift apart. That's why so many of the principles in this book center on building and maintaining personal relationships in business.

RAM recognizes that relationships are assets and takes the Relationship Web as a metaphor for the interconnected nature of these assets. With that recognition and that metaphor in mind, it's time to define Relationship Asset Management.

RELATIONSHIP ASSET MANAGEMENT

When we founded Systems Consulting Group, we set out to build a company that took relationship management to new heights. This was partly out of necessity: We were a new company, and, like most new companies, we had a small staff and modest resources. Perhaps we saw relationships as assets because relationships were pretty much the only assets we had. We knew, for example, that we didn't want and couldn't afford a large sales force or an expensive publicity program. So, we developed ways of leveraging off the sales forces of other companies and getting customers to agree up front to provide testimonials and to be covered in magazine articles (provided, of course, that the project was a success). We looked at our business goals and at our Relationship Web—including potential members of our Relationship Web—and systematically asked ourselves, "Who can help us achieve our goals, and how can we help them?"

On a practical level, people didn't help us just because they liked us. They helped us because we were consistently able to provide wins for them in exchange for the wins that they helped us to achieve. That win-win, or win-centric, element is the key feature of Relationship Asset Management. Mutual wins are also the key characteristic of a non-manipulative, nonexploitive business relationship. To our way of thinking, when a businessperson defines winning as beating the other guy in a deal or "coming out ahead" in a relationship, he has already set himself up to lose. His relationships can't last, nor can his reputation. The search for mutual wins places both parties on the same side of the table, working on the situation so that they both come out ahead rather than working each other over to get the upper hand.

For example, here's how we created a mutual win that enabled us to leverage off other companies' sales forces: After founding SCG, we knew that if we could get in a prospect's door, we would stand a good chance of making a sale because of our experience and expertise. The question was, "How do we get in the door?" We searched our Relationship Web and saw a potential asset in the software vendors out there. We decided to try to align ourselves with vendors working in hot areas at the time, such as financial systems, sales force automation, data warehousing, and enterprise resource planning (ERP). Those companies had sales forces already calling on the very customers we were targeting. We believed that we could leverage off their sales forces *if* we could find a win for those vendors.

A software company usually finds itself competing for a customer against two or three other firms with similar software. As part of the sales process, each company demonstrates its software for the prospective buyer, usually with canned data—Acme Corporation, widgets, fictitious numbers, that sort of thing. To give these companies a win—and a reason to introduce us to their prospects and clients—we offered to create for their salespeople in these situations, at no cost to them, a customized demo of the software using the prospect's data. That way, when the salesperson ran the demo, the prospect saw the software running with his company's data and the customized reports that his company would use, instead of the standard "Acme Corporation" data.

This gave the salesperson a serious advantage over her competitors at absolutely no cost. SCG spent several man-days tailoring the demo the way the salesperson wanted it, and we did it with no guarantee other than the introduction to her prospect. However, with what we learned about the prospect and about the software, we often converted the introductions into relationships. In fact, this strategy worked so well that we never needed a sales force. It became a cornerstone RAM technique, and we sold millions of dollars' worth of work to Fortune 1,000 companies this way.

Over time, we devised a systematic process for developing these kinds of strategies. Aside from recognizing that relationships are assets, the process of RAM broadly comprises four steps:

1. Evaluate relationship assets in light of the company's goals, success factors, and risks.
2. Assign or recognize an owner of each relationship.
3. Define wins for all parties in each relationship.
4. Move the relationship into the win-win zone, and keep it there.

A summary of each phase and the role it plays in RAM strategy follows.

STEP 1: EVALUATE RELATIONSHIP ASSETS IN LIGHT OF GOALS, SUCCESS FACTORS, AND RISKS

Developing a RAM strategy demands that management first do this:

- Define organizational goals.
- Assess the key success factors involved in achieving those goals.
- Understand all critical risks.
- Identify stakeholders who can help the company reach the goals, enhance the success factors, and mitigate the risks.

For RAM to work, you *must* make the tie between your relationship assets and your goals, success factors, and risks. Suppose, for instance, that your company has the goal of continued rapid growth and has decided that this involves the key success factor of "recruiting competent, motivated employees." In this first step, you might consider the following stakeholders and their (hypothetical) characteristics:

- **Current employees.** Your staff is among the most productive, lowest-turnover groups of professionals in your industry. When your employees recommend people, those people usually succeed.

- **Colleges and universities.** In your headquarters area, three universities annually graduate some 125 students with majors in specialties that you require. In addition, about 20 of these students come from nations where you do business or would like to do business.

- **Executive recruiters.** Three of your top ten technicians and five of your top ten sales reps came from two executive recruiting firms.

- **Regional and local media.** Your human resources department and your hiring managers have told you that interviewees still mention a negative article about your company that ran in the county newspaper a year and a half ago.

This list of stakeholders is hardly exhaustive, nor are the accompanying comments. Our intent at this point is to show the type of information to be developed on stakeholders and then assessed for its value in achieving goals, enhancing success factors, and mitigating risks.

That last point—mitigating risks—warrants emphasis. RAM helps you avoid costs, problems, and aggravation. So, in this identification and evaluation phase, ask yourself what it is worth to your company to avoid employee defections, supply shortages, government investigations, negative coverage, community protests, and the like. There's value in avoiding trouble, and it should be considered in any strategic evaluation of relationships.

STEP 2: ASSIGN AN OWNER TO THE RELATIONSHIP

Only the most antisocial among us would set out to destroy or squander a business relationship. Yet it happens. We mean that literally: It just happens, in the sense that it's passively allowed to happen. Most business relationships don't end with a conscious kiss-off or a knock-down, drag-out battle. Instead, they fizzle out or wither away. Or, as in the example of the snack and cereal company cited earlier, they end because a management decision hurts a relationship that no one adequately considered. Ultimately, however, in one way or another most business relationships that die do so because it's nobody's job to see that they live.

Therefore, management must make sure that the care and feeding of relationships is somebody's job. RAM strategy demands that someone be assigned as the owner of every relationship that was identified, evaluated, and prioritized in Step 1.

Step 2 determines who will own the relationship and who should be on the team that will manage that relationship. This could mean simply confirming an existing arrangement, or it might involve assigning a new owner and a new contact team to the relationship.

THE CHIEF RELATIONSHIP OFFICER

In our view, every organization needs a senior person responsible for the relationship environment—a chief relationship officer, or CRO, if you will. In Principle #3, "Create Ownership for Relationships," we will detail the role and responsibilities of this individual. For now, we merely point out that any sizable company has a senior manager responsible for every other class of assets—the chief financial officer, chief operating officer, chief information officer, and so on. If you believe that relationships are valuable assets requiring proactive management, as we do, you need a CRO.

Of course, no single individual can personally manage every relationship, even in a small organization. Therefore, the CRO must manage the company's relationship *environment.* This involves overseeing the entire RAM process, including the assignment of an owner to each relationship. Note that the CRO does not own the relationships with the stakeholders. He owns the environment in which those relationships are fostered and maintained.

The CRO also acts as the overseer and steward of these assets. Just as the CRO advises management on the company's financial status and the financial impact of decisions, he provides advice on the status of relationships and the impact of decisions on them. In the earlier case of the cereal company, if a CRO had been on the job, he would have pointed out that abruptly laying off seasoned salespeople would jeopardize relationships built up over time with store managers, and that those relationships were valuable assets. Those salespeople were the owners of customer relationships. The decision to lay them off created risks, which the CRO would have worked to eliminate or at least mitigate. The CRO also would have worked not necessarily to stop the lay-offs, but certainly to preserve the underlying relationships, perhaps by retaining the seasoned salespeople as consultants for a period of time or employing a phased-in approach to bringing in new salespeople.

In business, the things that get done are those that someone is directly responsible for getting done. That's why the CRO and relationship owners are so important to the success of RAM.

STEP 3: DEFINE WINS FOR ALL PARTIES IN EACH RELATIONSHIP

All relationships eventually produce one of four possible outcomes: win-win, win-lose (you win, they lose), lose-win (you lose, they win), and lose-lose. Only win-win relationships can endure. Therefore, because RAM seeks to maximize the long-term value of relationship assets, you must consistently find wins for all stakeholders on all sides of a relationship. This is why we call RAM a win-centric approach.

To craft a successful RAM strategy, you must consider the potential wins over the short term and the long term. This involves putting yourself in the other party's shoes through a process that we call spoking out, which we examine in Principle #5, "Move into the Win-Win Zone." It is also useful to ask the other party directly about the wins that it expects from the relationship. The goal is to make the wins explicit for everyone.

FROM THE RAM PLAYBOOK

Some people are reticent about discussing the wins that they expect from and will provide in a business relationship. These folks are sometimes shy or new to business, or they believe that it is crass to discuss what each party will get from a relationship. But being explicit about wins is the hallmark of seasoned professionals who realize that business is essentially a process of exchange, usually involving money. There are also nonmonetary wins in business, which we cover in Principle #5, and even those should be explicitly discussed. In business, it is okay to talk about money, to ask for what you see as fair (and to explain why you see it that way), and to question people when you believe that the wins are not balanced.

Finding the win typically means opening up your thinking about business relationships, getting rid of stereotyped notions, and considering all potential costs and benefits. For example, Starbucks Coffee Company chairman Howard Schultz looked beyond the usual ideas about company-paid employee benefit plans. Two thirds of Starbucks' employees are part-timers, a group usually not eligible for the full range of benefits at most companies. In fact, many fast-food, retail, and consumer services businesses deliberately employ a large part-time staff to reduce benefits expense. Starbucks, however, offered all benefits, including stock options, to all employees. The win for the employees is healthcare insurance and other benefits that they couldn't get elsewhere. The wins for Starbucks were lower employee turnover (in a high-turnover business) and decreased recruiting and training costs. The company ultimately made money, saved money, and became stronger—wins well worth the cost, in Schultz's view.

The wins need not always be that dramatic. Employees see wins in improved career opportunities, new skills, teamwork, or even a change of scenery. People want to feel good about their employers, and it's a win when they feel that way. GE Plastics, for instance, launched a Share to Gain program in which hundreds of employees worked on renovating YMCAs, homeless shelters, and similar nonprofit community facilities. The program created a triple win. The community won by getting improved facilities. The employees won by gaining a sense of satisfaction and accomplishment. The company won by racking up good-corporate-citizenship points and forging *esprit de corps* among employees.

Thinking about the long term helps a company keep relationships in the proper perspective. For instance, you might have to accept a lose-win situation in the short term to establish a relationship or to reestablish one that has slipped into the win-lose zone. That's fine. Short-term adjustments are often necessary. In the long run, identifying wins for all stakeholders in a relationship—and making those wins happen—is the essence of RAM.

STEP 4: MOVE THE RELATIONSHIP INTO THE WIN-WIN ZONE, AND KEEP IT THERE

In our consulting business at SCG, we tried to avoid just handing our clients an information technology strategy and leaving it at that. Our goal was to stick around for the implementation. Strategy without implementation is just words on paper. Moreover, RAM is not just a "strategy." It's a way of life. Every day, with every contact, your company moves relationships either toward the win-win zone or away from it. It either builds relationships or lets them wither. To work, RAM must be put into action.

Implementing RAM strategy requires a certain frequency and type of contact with various stakeholders. You must have systems for collecting and monitoring information on all elements of a relationship. The CRO, the relationship manager, and the contact team must communicate with one another regularly. This takes discipline, and it takes doing. However, the last thing we want you to think is that RAM is "just one more thing to do." Every company, every organization of any kind, already has relationships. Implementing RAM strategy usually means doing things that you're already doing, but doing them more effectively and with a longer-term view.

Your organization might have to break some habits. For instance, many companies will exploit a temporary advantage when the power in a relationship shifts in its favor due to supply-and-demand imbalances, new regulations, or luck. RAM strategy could call for *not* using the power of a temporary advantage over a stakeholder. Not exploiting that power can provide a short-term win for the other party and a longer-term win for you. People remember who takes care of them and who takes advantage of them when they're powerless. Put another way, people remember who their friends are.

By the same token, the simple act of being a friend in someone's time of need gives that person a win that won't be quickly forgotten, and often at little cost to you. Wouldn't you want the same kind of treatment and remember it? For instance, at SCG, when we heard that someone at a client of ours had lost his job through termination or lay-off, we were naturally concerned—and we acted on that concern. As you'll see, we generally took the trouble to get to know the people we worked with. We then would call to offer our sympathy and help in networking to find a new job and, what's more, access to a desk, a phone, and our photocopier. Relatively few people needed to take us up on that offer. As managers and professionals in a talent-strapped industry, they could usually find a new position in a matter of weeks. However—and this is the point—all of them said the same thing to us in so many words: "Thanks a million for calling me at a time like this, when I'm down on the mat. And thank you for offering to help."

The immediate win for the client (actually, *former* client at that point) was support at a time when anyone would want it. That gesture was not forgotten. How do we know? Because when those people found new jobs and needed IT consulting services, they hired or recommended us. They knew our work from their previous experiences with us. And they knew that we had their best interests at heart because we had offered them support when they needed it. So, our longer-term win was goodwill, an important component of any relationship asset.

Actions like that—they're not really "tactics" because you're simply acting on your own best impulses—represent the daily, on-the-job implementation of RAM strategy. Most of the principles in this book involve that kind of implementation. It comes down to thinking of the other person and his situation (as well as your own), seeking mutual wins, managing toward those wins, and acting on every opportunity to create wins on all sides. Instead of passively letting relationships hit or miss or grow or die, RAM strategy proactively builds relationships through this four-step process. It also turbocharges every organizational effort because relationships ultimately determine whether those efforts succeed or fail.

POST-GAME WRAP-UP

- A company's relationships are valuable assets because, like other assets, they enable the business to reach its goals.
- Every relationship the company has, even those with competitors and government agencies, is important.
- Relationships with former stakeholders should be viewed as assets.
- Every relationship must have an owner, or eventually it will die.
- Each company has a unique Relationship Web and therefore a unique set of relationship assets that cannot be appropriated, duplicated, or stolen.
- Relationship Asset Management is a systematic, win-centric means of initiating and building relationships that help companies and individuals reach goals, enhance success factors, and mitigate risks.

PRINCIPLE #2:

DEVELOP A GAME PLAN

Typically on Sunday night after a game, the offensive coaches go into one room to view reels of the next opponent's defense. The defensive coaches are in another room looking at the upcoming rival's offense. Each play is charted: down, yards to go, offensive and defensive formations …. The coaches use this information in putting together the game plan, which, for all the mysticism that surrounds it, is nothing more than a list of plays and defenses that are expected to work in certain situations.

—*From* The Hidden Game of Football, *by Bob Carroll, Pete Palmer, and John Thorn*

Relationship Asset Management grew out of our experience in building the Systems Consulting Group. We started with the basic idea of leveraging relationships but developed our game plans, so to speak, by reviewing our experiences, thinking them through and improving our approach to various stakeholders. Here we'll review some of the "plays" that we came up with in developing and executing our RAM strategy, and then we'll lay a foundation for your RAM game plan.

Looking back on the days when we started SCG, we knew that we had learned a lot about the consulting business during our years at Arthur Andersen Consulting (since renamed Accenture). However, like every start-up, we needed a strategy for growing the business quickly. We had zero brand-name awareness, no tangible assets to speak of, and no money to spend on marketing or salespeople. So we thought long and hard about how we could build the business without those resources.

Most consulting firms that we know of focus their relationship-building efforts on the buyer, on the executive who hires them and cuts their checks. We believe that the main reason most rank-and-file people on the client side resent consulting firms is that the consultants act as if the client's staff doesn't matter. They concentrate solely on making the buyer look good and keeping her happy.

We understand why consultants take that approach. Yet we wondered what the effect would be if, in addition to focusing on the decision-maker and check-cutter, we also made the client staff look good and developed relationships all the way down the line. What would that cost us? What would be the upside? We reasoned that, at the very least, we would find it easier to work with the client's staff. We wondered what other benefits might accrue. So we came right out of the box with the strategy of building strong relationships with buyers *and* with implementors, influencers, and support people on the client side. Our basic approach, the basic win we could give them, was to make them look good through our efforts. It was only a matter of time before we extended that approach to everyone we dealt with in our business.

That simple idea represented the first seedling of Relationship Asset Management. Before long that seed sprouted into the first tender, green shoot, and it happened as the (unforeseen) result of turnover on the client side. As you might know, managerial and employee turnover in IT outpaces that in most other functions. So, after we had been in business a while, people we had worked with at one client began to move on to other companies. When those buyers or decision-influencers needed IT consulting services, who do you think they called or recommended as good consultants? People they knew, people they had enjoyed working with—and people who had done a good job—at their previous employer.

One of our first clients was Burger King, headquartered in Miami. Before long, an IT manager moved from Burger King to Norwegian Cruise Lines and introduced us to his new employer. This led to an engagement and a relationship with Norwegian Cruise Lines. We saw this happen time and time again, and it was the earliest validation of our strategy. It also taught us an extremely important lesson: One introduction is worth 10 leads. We'll talk more about that later. Let's first get an overview of our RAM strategy at SCG.

EVERYONE, ALL THE TIME

A major league coach in any sport must work with the players, the assistant coaches and trainers, and the executives in the front office—the owner, president, and general manager. He also must consider the opposing teams and their coaches, the league management, the fans, and the media. All these constituencies play a role in the coach's success, and he must build good relationships with all of them, or at least as many of them as he can. Even relationships with opposing teams can be valuable, as in college sports, where many peer schools trade game films with one another. Let's say that Miami is playing Oklahoma this year but is not playing Nebraska, and the Nebraska-Oklahoma game comes up before the Miami-Oklahoma game in the schedule. If Miami has a good relationship with Nebraska, Miami's coach might be able to get the game films from Nebraska's coach, along with some insights on Oklahoma's game-day strategy. Of course, Miami will do the same for the Nebraska coach when Nebraska faces a similar situation.

Managers and entrepreneurs face an even wider array of relationships than the average coach. But they don't always realize it. As a result, most companies take way too narrow a view of the role that various relationships can play in their business. For instance, when considering ways to increase sales, they see only sales and marketing people and their customers and prospects as relevant. When looking to control costs, they enlist only employees, and perhaps suppliers. In contrast, RAM strategy considers *all* stakeholders and would-be stakeholders as *potentially* important in reaching a goal, enhancing a success factor, or mitigating a risk.

At SCG, we knew that we had to work effectively on the two sides that any business must manage: demand and supply. Every business faces the twin challenges of generating demand for its products or services and marshaling the supplies to meet that demand. Every business amounts to an infrastructure that serves as an intermediary between demand for what it sells and the supply of resources that it transforms to meet that demand.

For us, demand encompassed all the players in the marketplace for IT consulting services: prospects, customers, and anyone who might help us land consulting engagements—current and former customers, suppliers, other vendors, the media, charities, and the larger community. As with any consulting or professional services firm, the supply side consisted mainly of employees and prospective employees who could fulfill engagements on time, as specified, and within budget. We knew that to attract first-rate employees we could benefit from relationships in several quarters: current employees, former employees (the few that we had), customers, suppliers, universities, the media, charities, and the larger community. Even relationships with competitors could help by allowing us to fill holes in our skill set by hiring their employees as temporary contractors.

To place this in the context of goals, success factors, and risks, we offer the following subset of our overall plan:

- Our *goals* were to achieve rapid revenue growth and consistent profitability by winning consulting engagements (boosting demand) and building a solid staff to fulfill them (maintaining supply).

- Our *success factors* on the demand side included credibility, reputation, and entry to good prospects. Our supply-side success also depended on building a good reputation quickly and offering competitive pay and good working conditions.

- The major *risks* on the demand side were posed by more established competitors. The marketplace was crying out for IT services, so aggregate demand was no problem. But could we get in to see prospects, given all the competitors banging on their doors? Could we outmaneuver firms with existing relationships with our prospects? On the supply side, we faced the *risk* of being outdone in the search for talent by larger competitors with big reputations and the ability to match our pay and working conditions. Thus a major risk was balancing the supply of consultants with the demand for their services, neither overhiring nor underhiring.

RAM begins with examining all possible relationships in light of your goals, success factors, and risks. This means examining every stakeholder or potential stakeholder and asking two questions: "How can a relationship with this person or outfit directly or indirectly help our company, division, or department—or me as a professional—to achieve a goal, enhance a success factor, or mitigate a risk?" and "What can we do to provide wins for them, either proactively or in return?"

With SCG's goals, success factors, and risks in mind, we examined our Relationship Web and focused on the demand and supply sides of the business.

BOOSTING DEMAND

On the demand side, we believed that the major hurdle we had to over-come was establishing trust. As a new company, SCG needed credibility. We had the experience and the expertise in place, and we knew that the need for IT consulting services was strong. Therefore, we believed that if prospects trusted us, they would buy our services a viable percentage of the time. So, we asked ourselves, "How can we employ our major asset, relationships, to build trust and credibility?"

As the top executives of the firm, we brought in the earliest accounts through traditional selling—sales letters and phone calls, fol-lowed by onsite sales calls. Soon, however, our strategy of building rela-tionships with everyone on the client side bore fruit. In the early days, we focused chiefly on relationships with existing clients and the media, and then, as we mentioned in Principle #1, "See Relationships as Valuable Assets," we soon brought other vendors into the mix.

Here's how we built credibility based on our client relationships: Given our growth objectives, we needed a way of securing good, usable references from clients right from the start. In negotiating the contract for our services, most clients wanted a very predictable win—a reduction in our fee. This would be expressed in the usual ways: statements about tight budgets, cost control efforts, and difficulties getting approval for high-ticket work. Expecting this, we prepared some wins beforehand that we would be interested in receiving in return for a reduction in our fee.

The win that we wanted would cost the client nothing but would be extremely valuable to us. In return for the reduction in our fee, the client would agree—as part of our contractual arrangement—to do cer-tain things that would help us market ourselves. They agreed to become solid references for SCG and a source of quotes about the quality of our work—provided, of course, that our team performed properly. We would be allowed to write up a case study of the engagement to use in our marketing materials. If the engagement was particularly interesting, we could refer journalists to the client, and their management would take part in interviews. This, by the way, created a RAM trifecta: We won by getting positive, credible publicity, while the client also got good PR and the journalist got a lead to a good story.

When the engagement went particularly well, the client would write a complimentary letter on company letterhead about how well it had gone. As the firm grew, we had these letters matted and framed and displayed on a wall in our reception area to impress prospective clients, which they invariably did. These "job letters" were so valuable to us that we paid bonuses to the consulting team on any project that resulted in one. (There was even a joke at SCG that we would make people wait an extra few minutes in our reception area to give them time to read the letters on the wall—just a joke, of course.)

Moving further along our Relationship Web, rather than waiting "until we can afford it," we soon became involved with charitable organizations in South Florida. This created wins in several quarters. It helped us build trust within the community (another stakeholder that we always saw as important). It demonstrated to employees that they were working for a company that cared about the common good. It also, of course, assisted the charitable organizations. In six years, we raised and collected a total of $250,000 for the Miami Bridge, a home for abused and runaway children, and several other South Florida charities. We helped paint the Miami Bridge facility and make repairs. (We also built a basketball court and made the mistake of setting the rims at $10^{1}/_{2}$ feet instead of the regulation 10 feet. We might have done it on purpose as a practical joke if we had known how amused the kids would be when one towering 16-year-old couldn't make his dunks anymore and thought he'd lost it.) This kind of involvement created other wins as well. Our employees felt great about themselves, and the whole effort created some wonderful moments. We also received media coverage of our efforts. And we had a blast doing it, partly because our major fund-raising event revolved around golf with our friends, clients, and local personalities.

We were always aware of the role the media could play in building our business. Positive press coverage gives a company credibility that no amount of advertising can buy. Positive press coverage gives a company credibility that no amount of advertising can buy. (This is not a typo— it's important enough to say twice.) The issue is: How do you get coverage, particularly if you don't have a large public relations budget. Our strategy for getting media attention was to leverage our relationships with clients and with the charity we supported. That way, it's not just about us and our company. It's also about the clients and how smart they are and about the charity and the good work they do. The media outlet wins by having success stories on a new business and some good news to report. In addition, we would help with research or writing of the piece for free if the reporter or editor wanted assistance.

FROM THE RAM PLAYBOOK

Virtually all charities are doing work that's worthy of support. Therefore, it might seem that it doesn't matter much which one a company decides to approach. Or, it might seem that you should support a very well-known one. In our experience, it's better to consider this important decision from another angle.

Keep the strategic considerations in mind. You are doing this to be altruistic and to share your company's good fortune *and* to achieve visibility and goodwill in the community. Consider whether the charitable organization is one that your employees can support with their time and talent. Does the organization need volunteers? Can it benefit from the skills that your people offer? Would the charity's mission appeal to your employees? If so, your people will become more involved in the charity and more familiar with its work. They'll also enjoy more opportunities to strengthen relationships among themselves. Finally, try to choose a charitable organization that you feel you can stick with over time.

For all these reasons, it's best for many companies—particularly small companies—to "adopt" a relatively small charity. Your financial contribution will have greater impact, and the need for volunteers is usually greater than at larger, more established charities. These charities also usually have a greater need for publicity, so your organization and theirs can team up to draw media coverage. In addition, as you progress together, a strong bond can develop between a growing company and an expanding charitable organization. That relationship makes the wins easier to define and deliver.

Two caveats go with this: First, although this larger-fish-in-a-smaller-pond strategy can work well, a less-established charity can become dependent on a few relatively large contributors. So, you must be honest with yourselves and with the charitable organization about your ability to continue your support during a business reversal. Second, size alone should not be the only criterion. One of our current enterprises is headed by a senior executive with diabetes, so that company supports a local chapter of the American Diabetes Association. With his personal stake in the organization's work, that executive can be a particularly credible spokesperson and a motivated fund-raiser for the foundation.

These kinds of opportunities lay in every organization's Relationship Web. They're easy to locate, with the right questions: Who can help you reach a goal, enhance a success factor, or mitigate a risk—whether or not you currently have a relationship with them? How can an existing relationship help you form a new one? Who can help you, and how can you help them? Are there opportunities for three-way wins? Given that everything in business depends on relationships, it's essential to develop the habit of thinking broadly about your Relationship Web.

In Principle #1, we mentioned how we leveraged relationships with vendors to gain access to prospects. We'll say more about exactly how we did that when we discuss other principles later in this book. That strategy gave us an introduction, exposure, and experience with the prospect that positioned us to make sales in a way that no other method—or, at least, no other method we could think of—would. However, all of our efforts with the stakeholders cited previously contributed to our credibility and to prospects' awareness of SCG, and thus to our ability to make sales.

Those are the basic ways that we worked RAM strategy on the demand side, which has to do with bringing in business.

ENSURING SUPPLY

Any new company competing against larger, established firms must come up with creative ways of attracting and retaining talented employees. When we surveyed our Relationship Web, we discovered one of the most commonly overlooked assets—potential relationships with universities. Yes, most Fortune 500 companies conduct on-campus recruiting efforts at selected universities. Even more companies make sure that their materials are available in the university's job placement office. But we needed a more hands-on approach.

We knew that as SCG grew, we would be hiring a steady stream of people out of college and graduate school. So, we set out to develop relationships with universities in our area. We went beyond merely introducing ourselves to the people in the career development office and posting job openings on bulletin boards. We developed opportunities to speak to students on campus in forums on business and technology subjects, and one of us taught several classes in project management as a guest lecturer.

When we hired a recent graduate, we made him part of the team that maintained the relationship with that university. They called their professors as well as students who were going to graduate in the next class and told them that we would be recruiting on campus the following week and that they should definitely stop by to meet us. After our employee did campus recruiting for a couple of years, he passed the baton to an alumnus that we hired after him. That way, we always had a recent graduate on the relationship management team. Oddly enough, few of our competitors brought a recent grad back to recruit on campus.

This technique turned out to be more powerful than we anticipated (as was often the case with these early RAM strategies). Our recruiter got a win out of it because he got to show off his success and help bring a friend, or at least a fellow alumnus, into the company. SCG won because our recruiting table was one of the busiest in the place, and we had a pool of first-rate recruits. Occasionally, professors we had met on campus even called exceptional students to our attention. The university won by having a young, growing IT consulting firm recruiting on campus.

To this day, we believe in building strong relationships between businesses and business schools. As of this writing, we've had efforts underway for about a year to bring RAM strategy into the curriculum of business school programs, with excellent results.

One obvious source of talent in our Relationship Web was our current staff. We offered cash payments to any employee who recommended a job candidate to us who we hired. Current employees rarely recommend a substandard candidate or a poor fit to their employer. It would reflect badly on them, and the candidate would probably not be hired anyway, which hardly creates warm feelings between them. When it works out, however, the employee, the new recruit, and the company all win.

Of course, after a few years, our positive media coverage and solid client list—and those job letters from well-known companies hanging in the reception area—also helped us bring on new people. Motivated, growth-oriented people look for the same qualities in their employers because fast growth creates opportunities for challenging work, rapid advancement, and salary increases. Being named to *Inc.* magazine's list of the fastest-growing U.S. companies in 1992 and 1994 bolstered that image for us, and we and our employees worked hard to ensure that the reality was in line with the image.

In sum, we started small, both as a company and in RAM, no doubt about it. Developing RAM and formalizing the strategy took us several years. Yet the foundation of our success lay in viewing all relationships and potential relationships as assets right from the start and in strategically employing those assets to generate demand and supply to fuel the business. This involved defining our goals (ethical business practices, excellent working environment, rapid growth, and consistent profitability) and understanding the success factors both on the demand side (credibility and access to prospects) and on the supply side (talented, motivated employees) as well as the risks (larger, well-funded competitors). Then we had to look across our Relationship Web and assess those relationship assets in light of our goals, success factors, and risks—and then work to build win-win relationships with those people and entities. The execution involved applying the principles detailed in the rest of this book.

Although we don't examine it in depth until Principle #5, "Move into the Win-Win Zone," effective execution depends on providing mutual wins. If you win and the other party doesn't, you lose. So, we're taking pains to show that not only did SCG win, but the entities and people we worked with also won. When you formulate your RAM strategy, bear in mind that the other parties' wins are as integral to the success of RAM as your wins.

WHAT'S YOUR STRATEGY?

Enough about us (for now anyway). What about you? How can you begin to create a RAM strategy for your business or for yourself?

RAM stands apart from other approaches to relationship management in several ways, but the main distinction is the strength of the tie between relationships and the needs of the business. Thus you start crafting a RAM strategy by developing a clear understanding of the goals, success factors, and risks of the business and, as you would in formulating any strategy, by setting a timeframe. Useful questions include these:

Goals:

- What are our revenue, profit, and other financial goals for the next year, two years, three years, and five years?

- Where do we want to be in terms of market share, industry ranking, or competitive position in our area over the next one to five years?

- What kind of company do we want to be? What do we want to stand for in our industry, in the community, and beyond? Which values do we want to project most forcefully to our stakeholders?

Success Factors:

- What does the business need in human resources, skills, and organizational culture to meet these goals?

- Which tangible resources—cash, equipment, IT infrastructure, plant, land, and transportation—do we have, and which do we need to acquire to reach our goals? By when do we need them?

- What must we know about the market, the competition, and the business environment that we do not know now?

Risks:

- Which events, conditions, or problems in the past have hampered our company's progress toward its goals?

- What five things are most likely to go wrong with the marketing, financial, and operating plans we've developed to move us toward our goals?

- What if the economy tanks? What if our technology is superseded? What if our two largest competitors agree to merge?

These are only samples, but questions like these must be answered by management, whose job it is to set the company's direction, or by the individual in a one-person shop. Managers often ignore questions about success factors and risks, which results in "management by wave of the hand"—setting goals, communicating them to the troops, and hoping that people somehow rise to the occasion. The more complete and realistic the definition and analysis of goals, success factors, and risks are, the more useful RAM will be to your company.

IDENTIFYING THE CURRENT AND OPTIMAL RELATIONSHIP WEBS

The next task is to define both your current and your optimal Relationship Webs. The current web is just that—the one that you and your company (or your department) have developed up to this point. The optimal Relationship Web is the one that you need to achieve all goals, enhance all success factors, and mitigate all risks identified in the previous step.

Charting your current Relationship Web should be relatively straightforward, as long as you consider *everyone* that you have a relationship with or that you come in contact with or know as a result of doing business. Then extend the web to people and organizations outside of business: to charities, church and civic groups, alumni associations you're involved in, outfits you do business with on a personal level—general contractors, landscapers, auto dealers, and so on—and, finally, personal friends and family members. At this stage, cast a wide net and consider literally every person and entity you know.

Charting the optimal Relationship Web entails two additional steps: First, identify the people and entities that could help you achieve a win—reach a goal, enhance a success factor, or mitigate a risk—*if you had a relationship* with them. As you did in defining your current Relationship Web, you must cast a wide net at this point. Ask yourself, "Who could help us achieve this win if we knew them and could discuss the possibilities for mutual wins with them?" Second, identify which relationships people in your Relationship Web have that could help you achieve a win. With the right approach, you can make the Relationship Web of someone you know available to you. When someone knows someone who can potentially help you, that person belongs on your optimal Relationship Web.

Thus, in addition to relationships with people you *do* know, you're also considering potential relationships with people you *don't* know. Is it realistic to strategically consider relationships with people you haven't even met? Yes it is, thanks to the technique of RAM cultivation, which we cover in Principle #4, "Transform Contacts into Connections." Continually cultivating relationships at all stages means that you will always have early stage, maturing, and long-term relationships in your portfolio of relationship assets. You will also usually have at least some entities and individuals that you have identified as potential stakeholders, even though you have not yet initiated contact. To cast the widest net, you must chart your "perfect world" as well as your current Relationship Web.

As a result of this exercise, you will have mapped your current Relationship Web and your optimal Relationship Web. Thus, you have an "inventory" of your current relationship assets, and you've specified those that you ideally need to develop.

FROM THE RAM PLAYBOOK

Some people misconstrue Relationship Asset Management as an exploitative approach to others. However, the defining characteristic of exploitation is one-sidedness. Workers are exploited when they are not compensated fairly for their labor. Communities are exploited when companies use their resources and provide little of value in return. In contrast, RAM's defining characteristic is the pursuit of long-term, win-win relationships.

An exploitative mind-set can't work with RAM because it blinds you to opportunities. Asking only, "How can this guy help me?" narrows your point of view and short-circuits relationships. Most people know whether you're interested in their success or only in your own. The me-first mind-set quickly reveals itself. If someone can't help you at the moment but you can help them, grab the opportunity. If you don't, you've missed a chance to form a real connection, to start a win-win relationship—and to help someone out.

On the other hand, RAM is clearly a business strategy, a means of developing contacts and forming connections with people who can help you and your organization move forward. David Arnold, a retired vice president of Shipley, Inc., and now a Boston-based venture capital investor and philanthropist, looks back on his career and notes, "When I was young and starting out, I didn't have a mentor and didn't realize the importance of developing contacts. However, I soon saw that the people you get to know can make the difference between success and failure in business." After earning his MBA at Harvard Business School, he set out to develop relationships with people who might be able to help him and who he might be able to help in the future, although he didn't know the form that help would ultimately take on either party's part. David adds, "I've seen people who criticize others who purposely develop contacts, but it's a tremendously important part of doing business."

GAP ANALYSIS AND COST-BENEFIT ANALYSIS

Now you are in a position to assess the gap between your current relationship assets and the set that you need. This is similar to the needs-analysis for any other resource. In their planning process, most companies gauge the equipment, skills, and money required to execute the plan. We're suggesting that the same analysis be performed for relationship assets.

Assessing the gap between the current and required relationship assets—that is, between the current and optimal Relationship Webs—provides the motivation, at the individual and organizational levels, to implement RAM strategy. Most companies are already performing at least some of the tasks that comprise RAM. They already have stakeholders and owners for many relationships. Yet implementing RAM means investing greater effort in building relationships and laying out some money. The motivation and justification for these efforts and outlays must come from somewhere. Gap analysis provides that motivation and justification by highlighting what needs to be done—and the payoff for doing it.

For example, we knew that it would take effort and expense to build a relationship with local universities to improve our chances of recruiting recent graduates. We knew it would take the same to cultivate the local media to enhance our company's standing in the community. Highlighting the importance of these relationships and the way they would help us reach our goals helped motivate us to implement RAM strategies.

In fact, at SCG we got into cost-benefit analysis as well as gap analysis. We looked at the cost of hiring, paying, and managing a sales force and then weighed it against that of developing relationships with vendors and the media. We looked at the cost of advertising against that of discounting projects for clients willing to act as spokespeople for SCG and against the cost of bonuses to our consultants who drew "job letters" for their work. We weighed the cost of recruiting through normal channels (such as want ads and employment agencies) against that of developing relationships with universities and paying bonuses to employees who recommended successful new hires.

Gap analysis highlights the relationships that you need to develop. Cost-benefit analysis reveals that because RAM strategies leverage relationships, they enable the organization to reach goals, enhance success factors, and mitigate risks with less expense and greater effectiveness than run-of-the-mill methods.

RELATING RAM TO OTHER STRATEGIES

As a strategy, RAM focuses on specific needs of the business as intensely as a marketing, financial, or operating strategy does. RAM strategy also complements those traditional business strategies, just as they complement one another. Marketing and operating strategies are linked because they serve the two vital sides of any business—marketing strategies boost demand, while operating strategies marshal the supplies necessary to meet that demand. Financial strategies underpin both marketing and operating strategy in that expenditures and investments must support those strategies, and monetary returns must justify them.

Relationships support all three traditional strategies. We believe that no marketing, financial, or operating strategy can be considered complete without a RAM strategy in place. Why? Because various stakeholders are going to implement those strategies and be affected by them. Those stakeholders must be considered so that, when appropriate, they can be brought into implementation efforts and, when necessary, be kept from impeding those efforts.

In sports and in any other endeavor, a team with a solid strategy will outperform a team without one. Given the strategic importance of relationships, every organization needs a strategic approach to identifying, building, and managing them.

POST-GAME WRAP-UP

- Your Relationship Universe includes every person or entity you know. In addition, anyone who can help you achieve a win is a potential member of your Relationship Universe.
- When you evaluate stakeholders or potential stakeholders for their ability to influence your wins, keep an open mind, but make explicit decisions about their possible roles. Not every stakeholder can help with every win.
- Gap analysis charts the difference between an organization's current position and where it wants to be, as well as what relationship assets will be necessary to get there.
- Cost-benefit analysis weighs the cost of developing relationship assets against alternative methods of attaining objectives, and then considers the benefits of RAM strategy against traditional methods.
- No marketing, financial, or operating strategy can be considered truly complete without a RAM strategy in place because relationships will be instrumental in implementing any of those strategies.

CREATE OWNERSHIP FOR RELATIONSHIPS

Costello: What's the name of the first baseman?

Abbott: No. What's the name of the second baseman.

Costello: I don't know.

Abbott: He's the third baseman.

Costello: Let's start over.

Abbott: Okay. Who's on first.

Costello: I'm asking you—what's the name of the first baseman?

Abbott: What's the name of the second baseman.

Costello: I don't know.

Abbott: He's on third.

—*Bud Abbott and Lou Costello*

Who's supposed to do what with which stakeholder? "I don't know" is probably the answer you'll usually hear if you ask around. First, there are numerous stakeholders in most companies, particularly large companies, and not all of them are always recognized, let alone covered. Second, stakeholders can shift roles, acting as employees, customers, investors, and citizens in the same week—or same day. Finally, few companies have relationship owners for all stakeholders *and* someone (other than an extremely busy CEO) coordinating all their efforts.

Managing relationships might not be new, but the idea of owning them is, and everything in business starts with ownership. Anything that's critical to a company's success has someone in charge of it. With someone in charge, that element will receive the attention it needs. People in the company will believe that it's important and will know that they'll be held accountable for it. Moreover, the proper support for the people "on the field" will be there when they need it.

That's why the chief relationship officer (CRO) is so important.

It's a radical idea, we understand that. We're suggesting an addition to the executive team—at least, in large companies—and, in smaller ones, another task for a senior manager to perform. But the importance of relationship assets warrants this. They are every bit as important as financial assets, operating assets, and information, which are overseen, respectively, by the CFO, COO, and CIO.

The following story illustrates the importance of the CRO.

Several years ago, a marketing manager in a division of a Fortune 500 company distributed Cross pens as gifts to customers who were willing to try a new product. The promotion went well, until the marketing manager received a call from the marketing vice president in his division. The vice president had received a call from the division president, who had received a call from the CEO at corporate headquarters. That CEO had received a call from an irate member of the company's board of directors.

The board member was a senior executive at the manufacturer of Parker pens. Why, he wanted to know, was a company on whose board he sat distributing Cross pens to its customers when Parker also had a line of fine pens?

What's the big deal? We're only talking about a couple thousand pens. Well, the senior executive at Parker thought it was a big enough deal to call his fellow board member—the CEO—on it. That CEO thought it was a big enough deal to get the message down to the marketing manager. By then, of course, it was too late. Yes, the marketing manager would know better next time. But what a missed opportunity to provide a win for a board member and his company at no additional cost, and maybe at a savings, and to avoid an embarrassing situation.

Would the win have had much impact on Parker's business? No. That is exactly the point: Small wins count. Most businesspeople can come up with a sensible (if not always successful) relationship management tactic when a huge win is at stake. It's the small, everyday situations that call for consistent professionalism, coordination, and thoughtfulness.

The chief relationship officer provides all of that and more. He creates the relationship environment and gets the right information on stakeholders to the right people. In this case, the CRO at the division would probably not know about the new product promotion. But he would have ensured that the marketing vice president was aware of all entities with an important connection to the company—board members as well as major investors, suppliers, and strategic partners. Then the marketing vice president, who did know about the new product promotion, would have ensured that the marketing manager used Parker pens rather than Cross pens as the promotional gift.

This illustrates one of the many wins that a CRO can provide. In more significant situations, the wins involve large sums of money and relationships that determine the company's success or failure. Thus, the CRO works with relationship owners across the company to raise their awareness of relationships, develop and implement RAM strategies, create wins, and avoid relationship killers. Those relationship owners are equally important to successful RAM strategy. So, before examining the CRO's job in more depth, let's look at the rest of the team.

THE RAM TEAM

Everyone who has contact with a stakeholder is on that stakeholder's RAM team. The key individuals, however, are the relationship owner and the chief relationship officer.

Although we prefer the term "owner," relationship managers have been used in sales—along with sales teams—for decades. In addition, most large companies have a manager of supplier relations, usually the purchasing manager, and managers of employee, shareholder, media, and community relations. In most instances, someone already involved in the relationship with a stakeholder can be recognized, confirmed, or assigned as the relationship owner. This person should be the primary direct contact between the company and the stakeholder. Typical owners of relationships with various stakeholders include:

Stakeholder	Relationship Owner
Employee	Direct superior or human resources manager
Customer	Account manager or salesperson
Supplier	Purchasing manager (or head of the department using the product)
Investor	Manager of shareholder relations (or the CFO or CEO)
Strategic partner	Key senior managers at each company (or the CEO at each company)
Media	Director of Public Relations (or marketing vice president)
Community	Director of Community Relations (or marketing vice president)

In a large company many, if not all, of these owners are already in place. Small to midsize companies without this formal structure usually have someone who can be confirmed or appointed the owner for each stakeholder. Smaller companies also have a natural advantage that companies of all sizes must strive for—personal relationships. For instance, in a small company, every employee can see the CEO, at least occasionally, and the investors may know the senior managers personally and have a deeper interest in the company's long-term success than the average shareholder in a large public corporation. Large companies cannot really duplicate those relationships, but with the right owners in place, they can create tighter bonds with stakeholders than they ever could without owners.

WHO OWNS WHAT?

We believe that one designated owner per relationship works best, with the CRO as "co-owner." The CRO should not attempt to own the relationship or to be the primary contact. Still, she should have occasional direct contact, particularly with significant stakeholders. This will help her to understand the relationship and assist the relationship owner. It will also prepare her to step in during an emergency or provide continuity if the owner suddenly resigns. However, the owner should be the primary contact with the stakeholder.

The strongest relationships result from multiple contacts at various levels throughout both organizations. Interaction at levels above and below the relationship owner—such as the CEO and the CRO above the owner, and sales assistants and administrative assistants, below the owner—create more points of contact and bind the constituent closer to the company. Every win-centric contact strengthens the bond.

We've mentioned that we did this at SCG. Our client relationships were formed at the partner level (the highest level) of our organization and at the CIO or CEO level of the client. Our onsite consultants established relationships with their peers on the client side. Our support people did the same with their peers. We also formed interlevel bonds, for example, between our support staff and the client's midlevel people.

The four steps of RAM strategy represent the roadmap guiding everyone in this process. The CRO appoints or recognizes the owner, and together they evaluate the relationship in the context of goals, success factors, and risks. They also determine the mutual wins to be created over the period. Then the owner, with the CRO's guidance, implements the strategy. The owner sits in the pilot's seat following the flight plan worked out with the CRO. The owner operates the aircraft, monitors the instruments, and responds to changing conditions, calling the tower—the CRO—when necessary. Meanwhile, the tower watches the skies for rough weather and for opportunities to soar higher, and advises the pilot accordingly.

The owner will crash and burn without a good working relationship with the CRO. Success depends on common goals, respect for roles, mutual trust, and open communication the part of both parties. An owner who fails to develop relationships, ignores the CRO, or pretends he's on track when he isn't is as bad as a CRO who oversteps his role, cuts out the owner, or disrespects the owner's judgment. So, the relationship owner and the CRO are equally important.

FROM THE RAM PLAYBOOK

People do not coalesce into a team because someone calls them a team. People become a true team only when they're invested in one another's success.

Some years ago, a communications giant realized that its major customers were being called on by numerous salespeople from various divisions. A large account might deal with someone from four different divisions in the same week. To make life easier for customers and more profitable for the company, management appointed high-level relationship managers (RMs) to oversee and coordinate the entire relationship between the company and major customers.

In effect, the parent company told each division, "So-and-so is now the RM for your customer, XYZ, Inc. We want your salespeople to cooperate with him." And—you guessed it—the salespeople did not cooperate with the RMs, who found their positions phased out a year later.

A number of things went wrong: First, the parent didn't create mutual wins. What were the wins for the divisional salespeople? Rather than wins, they lost their autonomy and, quite possibly, standing with their customers. Thus, they viewed the RMs as a threat. Second, with nothing but a mandate from on high, the RMs couldn't justify their role, which was analogous to a "Sales CRO." Third, they had no real preparation for the role.

Finally, there was no strategic approach to relating the RMs' activities to the goals, success factors, and risks of the divisions. The RMs were supposed to review contracts across the divisions and tag along on sales calls to create "synergy" between divisions, but that was too vague an objective. Worse, it did nothing to help the divisions hit the revenue and profit targets that the parent company was still holding them to.

RAM principles would dictate scuttling this program before it was launched—or ensuring that the success of the RMs and the success of the divisional salespeople (and managers) were linked in win-win fashion. Also, there would have to be clearer wins for customers.

At a high level, the RAM team extends horizontally across the company—that is, all of those in-place relationship managers for customers, suppliers, employees, shareholders, the media, and the community must see themselves as a team. They also need to view their stakeholder groups as borderless fields to be cultivated and harvested rather than silos of grain to be hoarded. The CRO must work to create this consciousness, which eliminates "turf wars." The managers maintain their traditional reporting lines rather than reporting to the CRO, but the CRO evaluates them on their stewardship of their relationship assets.

OWNERSHIP IN ACTION

In the early years at SCG, one of us owned a given client relationship. As we grew larger, project managers became the owners while we handed the job of CRO off to one another. We also tried to establish multiple contacts between our people and everyone we could on the client side. This is essential to a long-term relationship, particularly in a high-turnover business. As noted, we developed multiple contacts in most cases but were particularly successful at Burger King, our first large client.

How did we do it? We went out of our way to deliver timely, high-quality work to the IT group—and to work closely with the users. If a user (of the client's IT services, such as a manager in the marketing, accounting, or human resources departments) had an urgent request, we took care of it as quickly as we could. If a human resources manager needed a report generated—say, a readout of all employees who received training in the past six months—we put one of our programmers on the task and got it done. This was a win for the user because, instead of having to wait in the queue of IT projects, she got her report the next day. The folks in IT got a win out of it because we took bricks out of their wheelbarrow. And SCG won by making new connections throughout the company.

This had three effects: First, we increased the value that we delivered to the client. Second, the users came to know us and enjoy working with us. Third, SCG was the only IT consulting firm to last there as long as we did—the full eight years that we owned the company. During that time, the CIO position saw lots of turnover. Usually, a new CIO either stops using consultants or brings in a firm that he already knows and trusts. (We certainly understand *that*.) But the IT staff and users lobbied to keep us on board because we understood the users' needs and did everything we could to fulfill them.

Were we able to establish so many points of contact at every client? Unfortunately, no. It's just not always possible to have so many people working so closely with a client. In this case, the relationship management team spread far and wide and was still able to do a great job.

At universities, after we were up and running, the relationship owner was a recent graduate of the school. That arrangement gave the university a comfort level, increased our credibility with potential job candidates, and ensured both continuity and current knowledge when one owner handed things off to a more recent graduate who served as the next owner. With employees, we were the owners in the early years. As our staff grew larger, individual project leaders became owners as well.

We're willing to bet that in your company, as in most, there are relationships—including some with key stakeholders—that have no owners. Others will have only one point of contact. The most effective relationship management teams have all three elements: a recognized owner, multiple points of contact, and a CRO, or someone who at least fills that role.

WANTED: CHIEF RELATIONSHIP OFFICER

The CRO's job in RAM resembles the CFO's in financial management and the CIO's in information management, with responsibilities specific to the mission. Broadly, the CRO is this person:

1. Owner of the relationship environment

2. Co-owner of the company's relationships

3. Architect of the RAM strategy

4. RAM missionary, teacher, and coach
5. RAM adviser and troubleshooter

The CRO is the *owner of the relationship environment* in that he creates the space, so to speak, in which relationships are managed as assets. The environment dictates everything from the RAM strategies that relationship owners pursue to the way people think about and treat stakeholders. The CRO's presence tells everyone that the company is committed to Relationship Asset Management.

The CRO *co-owns the company's relationships*. He knows their history and status. If a relationship owner suddenly leaves, the CRO works to minimize the risk of "orphaned" customers, suppliers, creditors, or charities. He eases the transition to a new owner. As co-owner, the CRO brings continuity to the relationship.

The CRO is the *architect of the organization's RAM strategy*. In this capacity, he helps management at all levels to identify the Relationship Web and to use relationship assets to achieve goals, enhance success factors, and mitigate risks. He ensures that the entire company is aligned with the RAM strategy, and he monitors implementation.

As *RAM missionary, teacher, and coach,* the CRO must first exemplify the principles of Relationship Asset Management and then instill those principles in the organization. Making everyone RAM-savvy entails formal training regarding relationship assets, their importance to the company, and RAM practices. Presentations, classes, videos, retreats, and interactive learning can all play a role in this effort.

As *RAM adviser and troubleshooter,* the CRO is the chief lobbyist and ombudsman for the interests of all internal and external stakeholders. As noted in Principle #1, "See Relationships as Valuable Assets," a CRO would have advised senior management at the snack and cereal company that laying off seasoned salespeople might negatively affect relationships with store managers—and sales. A CRO would have advised Microsoft management that, given its market share, the company should build relationships with competitors and with the government. As troubleshooter, the CRO is an on-call, in-house consultant on troubled relationships. The CRO sits on any committee dealing with emergencies such as oil spills, strikes, takeovers, regulatory conflicts, product liability, or criminal proceedings. If such a situation arises in the context of a strong win-win relationship, management will find it far easier to address. If that relationship exists, it's because the CRO did his job well, and he'll probably be equally valuable during the emergency.

Ultimately, a good CRO makes each person in the company the CRO of his own Relationship Web. This brings RAM to its fullest fruition. No one person, either owner or CRO, can implement RAM strategy on his own. The company needs the support of the CRO, and the CRO needs the support of the company.

Incidentally, if the notion of a CRO seems extravagant, consider that the chief information officer wasn't necessary until companies understood that information and knowledge constituted competitive advantage. More recently, companies have appointed chief privacy officers, or CPOs, to guard customer information and other data. On February 12, 2001, *The New York Times* reported that there are at least 100 privacy chiefs in the United States, a number expected to exceed 500 within a year. IBM, AT&T, Eastman Kodak, American Express, and Microsoft all have established the position. The CPO oversees privacy training, monitors compliance with privacy laws and regulations, and develops company privacy codes, among other duties. Mary Culnan, a professor of management at Bentley College, says that American Express "views privacy as a source of competitive advantage."

Privacy is clearly important, and, at the risk of crowding the executive ranks, we submit that a company's relationships represent an equally important, if not more important, source of competitive advantage.

CRO: POSITION OR A ROLE?

A chief relationship officer is ideally a distinct senior management position, although this ideal might not be possible initially. For whatever reason, a company might need to cast a senior manager with other responsibilities in the role of CRO. The position-versus-role decision depends on three factors:

- Size and complexity of the organization
- Size and complexity of the Relationship Web
- Availability of an executive with the skills and the willingness to accept the responsibility

The size of an organization determines the scope of the CRO's responsibilities and the structure of the job. In a large company, the CRO should be a true senior management position, reporting directly to the CEO. Designing and guiding RAM strategy in a large company is too large of a responsibility for a part-time CRO. Medium-size firms with relatively limited resources might feel that they can combine CRO responsibilities with public relations or human resources duties. Although these areas might appear to overlap with RAM, this arrangement is far from optimal. Establishing a separate CRO position boosts corporate growth. To benefit significantly, even small companies should give the overall responsibility to a single executive who believes in RAM and has the skill and stature to do the job. In a small company, the owner might be the only person who can act as CRO. In a midsize firm, it might be the head of advertising, human resources, or marketing. Whoever takes the position or role of CRO must understand the responsibilities and be committed to executing them—and be qualified for the position, of course.

Given our commitment to RAM, we've made sure that Adjoined Technologies, Inc., a consulting firm that we've invested in and advise, employs a full-time CRO. Helen Gomez, a founder of Adjoined and whose business card reads "Chief Relationship Officer," oversees Adjoined's relationships and fulfills the functions outlined in this chapter. As CRO, Helen co-owns relationships with portfolio companies, Entente (which has been renamed Adjoined Investments), universities, banks, suppliers, employees, customers, and the media. "Being chief relationship officer frees me to focus on relationship assets and work on them with everyone in the company and externally," Helen says. "The awareness you develop as a CRO definitely helps you to see opportunities to increase value that you or the relationship owners would not otherwise see."

FROM THE RAM PLAYBOOK

RAM *can* work almost too well. A year and a half ago, we set up a company called Entente (the French word for "alliance") to invest in IT consulting firms. Entente's first investment was in creating Adjoined Technologies. Then we set out to invest in other IT consulting firms. The original model was to have Entente as the holding company and investment arm, and to have Adjoined and other firms in the portfolio. These firms would share resources and leverage one another's relationships, and, we hoped, reach a point at which they would want to merge after "dating" one another. Then, down the road, they could be either sold individually, merged and sold as a unit, or taken public individually or as a unit. We believed that, although most people would view these firms as competitors, we could create an environment in which they could identify and develop mutual wins in many situations.

We identified and formed relationships with entrepreneurs and investors at recently founded or seed-stage consulting firms. When we explained RAM and our model, we found that most of them quickly grasped the concept. We say that RAM worked too well because the companies turned out to be so synergistic and well-matched that the "dating" periods proved very short. We acquired four more early stage companies, which rapidly merged into Adjoined, and a fifth one that is (as of this writing) still separate. This represents fruition of our strategy, but we had no idea that it would occur so quickly that we would wind up with a portfolio of only two companies in 18 months.

THE PERFECT CRO

There's no clear-cut career path to the CRO position, and graduate schools of business offer no courses in Relationship Asset Management, although we're working to change that. Therefore, candidates for the job must come from another function. Given the nature of the job, the person should be selected as much for personal qualities as for professional experience. The following five qualifications are essential.

First, the CRO must possess character, integrity, credibility, and professionalism. This is a high-visibility, high-impact position. The CRO navigates all levels of the organization, so she must command people's trust and respect, put people at ease, and quickly gain their confidence. She must be able to discuss touchy issues frankly without giving offense, and she must be a good listener. The CRO will be privy to sensitive information about corporate secrets, plans, mistakes, and careers. Some people are better equipped than others to handle such information.

Second, the CRO needs a proven ability to develop and manage business relationships. The ideal CRO loves doing business and genuinely likes people and wants the best for them. With this outlook, she is comfortable saying, "Look, here are the wins that I would like to achieve, and here are the wins that I see for you. We might discover more wins or different wins by the time this meeting is over. What do you think?" In addition, networking skills and a facility for bringing people together help tremendously. Yet, a "people person" in the warm-and-fuzzy sense isn't necessarily the best choice. The CRO must thrive on the business dimension of human relations. The position exists to create win-win relationships, not to satisfy the needs of a social butterfly.

Third, a good CRO would be a good manager and must have held a previous senior-level post. This enhances credibility and ensures that the CRO has experience and insights to offer senior and middle managers. In a small firm, a CRO will have a small staff (if any), but in a larger outfit she'll need support commensurate with the size and scope of the company. The necessary administrative skills would be hard to acquire on the job.

Fourth, a CRO should have broad, deep knowledge of the company and its industry. The more intimately the CRO knows the company's strengths and weaknesses, the less time she'll spend on the learning curve. Knowledge of current technology, organizational structures, motivational tools, and best practices would be a plus. So would the habit of quickly tapping those who know what she doesn't—colleagues, consultants, or academics.

Fifth, the CRO should view problems dispassionately, without resorting to blame, retribution, or self-aggrandizement. This person needs maturity of mind, an ability to keep things in perspective and to help others do the same. Seeing the big picture and being able to soothe emotions are success factors here, as is a respectful, nonconfrontational, team-building approach. Some people can fake this in an interview, but it cannot be faked on the job. Thus, the CRO should be a known quantity, probably promoted from within. Promotion from within is not essential, but the job can't be given to a potential loose cannon.

By that token, several characteristics disqualify a person from the position: insensitivity, inflexibility, arrogance, excessive ambition, ruthlessness, contempt for others, lack of patience, quickness to anger, a tendency to overpromise or exaggerate, and an outsized ego, mercurial temperament, or overly critical nature. Some of these attributes are tolerable—and occasionally useful—in a CEO or entrepreneur. In a CRO, any of them could be disastrous, which raises a point. If the perfect candidate for CRO is not available, and that could well be the case, it is better to compromise on knowledge and experience, which are more easily acquired than integrity or a new personality.

A senior manager we know at a major financial institution, who characteristically wants to remain anonymous, would be a terrific CRO. He partially fulfills the role in dealing with many of his bank's most complex and sensitive commercial accounts. Here's how admiring colleagues describe Jim (as we'll call him) when asked, "What's his secret?":

"If you went to a ball game with Jim and he had a stranger sitting to his right, by the third inning he would know the guy's name, his business, where he lives, and three other facts about him—not because he's trying to sell the guy anything, but because he just can't let a guy sit there without getting to know him."

Now that just shows that Jim likes people and can draw them out. The next colleague really nailed it: "I've been in a roomful of people from an account where we've screwed something up. I mean angry people, ready to shout us down and take their business out the door. Jim comes in, and right away they calm down. I've seen it in their body language and their faces. It's like, 'Oh, Jimmy's here. He's going to straighten this out. It'll be all right.' And then the meeting I thought would be a bloodbath ends with them ready to work with us and give us time to get back on the beam. It's all in the way he deals with people."

Have you ever known a Jim? We hope you have, because he's got what we can't really convey in the CRO qualifications. He's also got something that can't be learned from a book. Get a Jim as your CRO, and you're more than halfway there.

DELICATE MATTERS

Organizational life being what it is—territorial, resistant to change, and riddled with hidden agendas—the CRO will have a busy, challenging, and at times unpleasant job, even with the right personality and qualifications. When a company appoints a CRO, some people will respond negatively. Relationships are personal. Therefore, the CRO could be viewed as unnecessary or intrusive, or both. (Recall the case of those RMs at the communications giant.) People might ignore him or use him as a scapegoat. Even if he's heartily welcomed, he must quickly prove his worth or risk losing that goodwill.

The CRO oversees an area of job performance that has never been systematically examined. He helps hold employees accountable for a task that they're used to ignoring or explaining away—their management of relationship assets. This invites suspicion, resentment, and even sabotage. The situation becomes even more interesting when the CRO must confront his peers or superiors. The success of the position, therefore, depends heavily on the person who fills it.

Success also hinges on support from the CEO and other executives. The necessary alignment occurs only through a series of candid, senior-level discussions. In these talks, people can air their concerns, agree on objectives, and commit to move forward with one voice and vision, at least publicly. At a minimum, all of senior management must believe that relationships are assets worth developing and that someone must be responsible for the task.

On a brighter note, most people want to excel, and the CRO will help them do exactly that. Therefore, it's useful to position the CRO as one would a physician, psychologist, personal trainer, or golf pro—as an expert who can help. When people seek expert assistance, they realize that they are behaving wisely. The act of getting help when it's needed generates a sense of relief, well-being, and, ultimately, control. The CRO must understand this and capitalize on it.

In her dealings with relationship owners, the CRO must stay "on message" with regard to achieving goals, enhancing success factors, and mitigating risks. The CRO and RAM have one goal: to grow the company by maximizing the value of relationship assets. RAM is not an exercise in being nice for the sake of being nice. It's a strategy for binding valuable employees, customers, suppliers, partners, lenders, investors, and other stakeholders to the company for mutual benefit.

Despite all that's involved in having a CRO, we've found that the advantages and returns warrant the effort. A company's relationships are unique, and although they cannot be duplicated, stolen, or neutralized, they can be ignored, mismanaged, or lost. The CRO ensures that that doesn't happen and that these assets attain their fullest value.

OWNING UP TO IT

RAM strategy will turbocharge the company's relationships, but only to the extent that someone implements it. In either a full-time position or a part-time role, the CRO oversees implementation.

Young companies that start out without a chief marketing officer or a chief financial officer soon realize that they need one. What happens when the right person assumes either of those positions? Marketing or financial management rises in priority. It becomes more systematic and sophisticated. Managers receive better information on their customers and budgets, and can therefore make better marketing and financial decisions. Managers and employees see that the company has reached a new level of maturity and seriousness of purpose.

A CRO has the same effect, only with respect to relationships with stakeholders. This provides a strong advantage to the company, in both absolute and competitive terms. In that sense, the CRO is a secret weapon, backstop, and equalizer. No company that wants to maximize the value of its relationship assets can afford to be without one.

- To get anything accomplished in an organization, you must have someone accountable for it. Thus, the relationship owner and the chief relationship officer are accountable for implementing each RAM strategy.
- The relationship owner—usually the main contact with the stakeholder—"owns" the relationship asset, while the CRO owns the relationship environment.
- The CRO "co-owns" the company's relationships and is the primary architect of its RAM strategy. He also acts as RAM missionary, teacher, coach, adviser, and troubleshooter.
- To realize the fullest benefits of RAM, a company should appoint a full-time CRO. If that's not possible or the company is very small, a qualified senior manager can fill the role.
- Knowledge of the company and its business and stakeholders is extremely important but is not an essential qualification in a CRO. Essential qualifications include maturity, integrity, ability to communicate, ability to balance emotions, a genuine interest in people, and the ability to create mutual wins in business situations.

TRANSFORM CONTACTS INTO CONNECTIONS

One afternoon, during Andre Dawson's 1987 MVP season, he was in right field in Wrigley Field and the Cubs were clobbering the Astros, 11 to 1. In the top of the sixth inning Dawson ran down a foul fly, banging into the brick wall next to the foul line. In the seventh inning he charged and made a sliding catch on a low line drive that otherwise would have been an unimportant single. When asked after the game why he would risk injuries in those situations when the outcome of the game was not in doubt, Dawson replied laconically, "Because the ball was in play."

—*From* Men at Work: The Craft of Baseball, *by George F. Will*

That's the kind of dedication and hustle that people bring to their on-the-job interactions when they see relationships as assets. The ball is in play every time the phone rings, every time they sit down to a meeting, and every time they meet someone new. They know that every interchange can move a relationship forward or move it backward. They don't slack off because the customer is small, the employee has been around forever, the supplier depends on them for business, or the reporter is from a low-circulation newspaper.

Winners are defined by what they make of the opportunities available to all of us. In our business and social lives, we all come in contact with a broad range of individuals and institutions. Yet some of us never seem to connect with these people. Reasons include the pace of business life, the time crunch we're all under, or, in some cases, lack of social skills. These obstacles can be overcome if you recognize the importance of other people to your success—and realize that you bring something of value to business relationships.

Failure to connect means missed opportunities and undeveloped relationship assets, as in these situations:

- A seasoned loading-dock supervisor who knows the operation inside-out takes early retirement to care for his ailing wife. When he leaves, he's gone, never to be seen or heard from again.

- A reporter does a bang-up job covering the opening of the company's new headquarters. An administrative assistant in the company's publicity department clips and files the article, but no one follows up with the reporter or her editor.

- At a dinner party, a CEO is impressed by a young dentist starting up a private practice about a mile from headquarters. The executive enjoyed talking with the dentist, but the contact ends there because the company has no dental plan.

- A local university announces new courses in a field related to the company's business. Several executives discuss this at lunch and agree that it's "interesting" and leave it at that.

Each of these contacts represented a potentially rich relationship. Yet that potential cannot be realized until two or more people make a connection. Therefore, the fourth principle of Relationship Asset Management encourages us to transform contacts into connections and, ultimately, into relationships.

THINK LIKE A PLAYER

Although being a friendly and outgoing person helps, those characteristics do not ensure success with RAM. Instead, success depends on thinking in a certain way about the people you meet. Right from the start, whenever you meet someone, you must be actively thinking about ways for you to help that person realize a win and for him to help you toward one.

The mind-set of seeking mutual wins could produce the following effects in the examples cited previously:

- The shipping department comes up short-handed before the Christmas rush. The director of human resources knows the perfect temporary worker: the retired loading-dock supervisor. The man is available because the company never lost touch with him. The human resources department implemented an alumni contact program that keeps the company in touch with retirees.

- An environmental group has mounted a protest against the company's new production facility, and management needs help getting its story across to the public. Because the chief relationship officer coached the public relations department on RAM strategy, the department has a relationship with the reporter who wrote that great story when headquarters opened and with her editor. So, the CEO can invite the reporter to visit the facility with him and the chief engineer to see their side of the situation.

- After meeting the young dentist, the CEO ponders the possibility of a mutual win. He talks with his benefits manager about a partnership with the dentist. As a result, the dentist agrees to provide dental care for all employees at a reduced rate. This jump-starts his practice, helps employees, and gives management a chip in the next round of compensation negotiations.

- The vice president of human resources took action when she heard about the university's new courses. She visited the school's director of career development about a potential arrangement. Consequently, the company will accept five interns a year in a work-study program. The company lands interns and potential job candidates, the university can now state that it provides "real-world" experience, and the students get that experience plus a shot at full-time employment—a win-win-win triple play.

Everyday interactions represent potential relationships, assets that can either be lost forever or developed to enrich everyone involved. "RAM consciousness" keeps you alive to these possibilities. When you see one of them, it's time to take action.

The principle of transforming contacts into connections goes well beyond capitalizing on chance meetings. It also operates on a more strategic level, enabling you to ignite relationships with potential stake-holders you have identified. In planning a RAM strategy, you've assessed your goals, success factors and risks, and your current Relationship Web. You've also identified people you want to bring into your Relationship Web. Now the task of building relationships with those parties begins. How do you do that? How do you make contact? How do you turn those contacts into connections and then into relationships? How do you cultivate relationships? This principle shows how to go about it.

PREGAME PREPARATION

Before a game, an NBA coach spends hours studying tapes of previous games with the upcoming opponent. He weighs the strengths and weaknesses of both teams and works out match-ups, strategies, and plays. The coach does this beforehand so that his team can play to its strengths, neutralize the opposition, and respond quickly to changes as the game unfolds. The game plan plays out spontaneously, thanks to the pregame prep.

Preparation heightens your chances of making the most of a contact with a potential stakeholder. Research on a potential stakeholder should begin as soon as you've identified him. On the basis of that research, you can plan for the first contact before you initiate it. (If you meet someone by chance, you don't have that luxury unless the person happens to be on your list of desirable stakeholders. If that's the case, you should have done some research, just in case.) Research means gathering all the information you can about the potential stakeholder. Planning means using that information to formulate your approach and follow-up.

Here's research at its best: In high school (we remember), the first task of a young man in love is to learn everything possible about the object of his affection. Where does she live? How does she get to school? Who are her friends? Where's her locker? What does she like? Is she seeing anyone? This hunger for knowledge springs from a desire for contact and connection. Answers to these questions increase the probability of a "chance" meeting and a successful start of a real (as opposed to imagined) relationship.

In RAM, information should be gathered with the impassioned intensity that a young Romeo would bring to the task. We're not talking about snooping or stalking. Nor are we suggesting that you rifle desk drawers, hire detectives, or interrogate acquaintances. We're recommending a healthy curiosity about the organization or person you want to be in business with.

People who earn their living by turning contacts into connections know the value of research. An executive recruiter we know compiles a veritable dossier on short-listed candidates for a senior management position before telephoning any of them. She knows everything that would be on a resumé if the individual had sent one in (which they rarely have). That's the starting point. She and her researchers gauge candidates' strengths and weaknesses, salaries and potential for advancement at their current employers, their living situations and past addresses, and the schools, clubs, and charitable and artistic organizations they're involved in. This recruiter seeks mutual acquaintances—including executives she has previously placed in other positions—who might be able to supply information and perhaps introduce her to the potential candidate.

That's the research. In planning, the headhunter anticipates the objections that the candidate will make when she approaches him. Every candidate at first says that he's happy in his current position, whether or not it's true. The recruiter must have an idea of what might make this person even happier. Her research has already given her the answers to the basic questions: How long have you been in your current position? What are your responsibilities? What's your total compensation (roughly)? Which positions have you held in which industries? Therefore, she doesn't need to ask those questions, which the candidate would view as intrusive anyway. This frees the recruiter to prepare questions designed to spark a conversation: With your children now grown, have you considered a move to the Southeast? You're working in a solid industry, but would you be curious about an opportunity in one that's growing much faster? Your division was not sold in that attempted acquisition last year, but it could happen next time—may I tell you about an open position with greater stability?

In RAM, information gathering continues during the initial contact, over the next several contacts, and beyond. For an initial meeting, research places you further up the learning curve. In some situations, premeeting research is a necessity. For instance, approaching a potential customer without understanding his business, or an investor without profiling the deals he pursues, or a government agency without knowing its agenda can be a relationship killer.

Typically you'll need to develop specific information on both the organization you've identified as a potential stakeholder and the individual(s) you want to approach in that organization.

ORGANIZATIONAL INFORMATION

Before and during the early stages of a relationship with an organization, you should learn this information:

- **Basic facts.** Industry, products, and services; locations and regional coverage; sales, profits, major expenses, and significant assets and liabilities; major investors; alliances, partnerships, and equity connections with other enterprises; legal structure; and current and historical stock prices, if the company is public.

- **Historical information.** Who founded the company; when and for what purpose; key changes and events, such as mergers and divestitures; and major successes and failures.

- **Goals and situation.** Business and financial objectives, mission statement, reputation, regulatory issues, competitive position, strengths and weaknesses, chief competitors, and current problems and risks.

- **Management and personnel.** Biographies of senior executives, makeup of workforce, corporate culture, and hiring criteria.

Much of this information is readily available, especially on publicly held companies. The Web site of any organization is a good starting point. Sites linked to an outfit's Web site can point to other material, as can search engines such as Yahoo!, Lycos, Ask Jeeves, Dogpile, and About.com. Other useful sources include annual reports, SEC filings, press releases, and articles (which you can search for in the Lexis/Nexis and Dow Jones online databases, and online and offline in *The Wall Street Journal, The New York Times,* other major market newspapers, and business and special-interest magazines). For privately held companies,

Dun & Bradstreet provides the broadest coverage. Also, the public relations efforts of many private companies have generated articles that can be accessed.

Sometimes you'll find a Web site run by a disgruntled employee or an upset customer that details the company's real or imagined offenses. These sites operate without editorial oversight or journalistic standards, so take them with a grain of salt. Nonetheless, they—and the company's response to them—can be revealing.

Pursue any firsthand information available from your Relationship Web. Do you have suppliers or customers in common? Do you know former employees? How about reporters or securities analysts who follow the company? In important situations or under tight deadlines, an information broker or professional researcher can be quite useful.

At a minimum, research will tell you whom you're dealing with and will enable you to gauge the desirability of a relationship. The exercise will also increase your confidence and help you think clearly about potential wins for the other party. As a bonus, contacts you make with researchers, librarians, analysts, brokers, or reporters during the process will enrich your Relationship Web.

PERSONAL INFORMATION

In every phase of RAM strategy, you are actually dealing with people, not organizations. Therefore, you must also research the individuals you will be approaching. Basic information about senior managers is available from the World Wide Web, *Who's Who,* and SEC filings. If the person has published books, check out online bookstores such as Amazon.com. For articles, search a good database of periodicals, such as ABI/Inform from University Microfilm. However you go about gathering it—and, for most of it, the person himself will be the best source—the following information will eventually be necessary:

- **Job situation.** Responsibilities, size of staff, length of service, date of last promotion, relations with boss and co-workers, strengths and weaknesses, reputation, and attitude toward the work.
- **Experience and education.** Former employers, positions, and locations; high school, college, and graduate school; areas of study; technical training; and attitude toward employers and schools.
- **Family and living situation.** Marital status, name of spouse, names and ages of children, town of residence, home situation, commuting situation, and make of car.
- **Other key information.** Important achievements; favorite sports teams, hobbies, and pastimes; political affiliation; status of health; eating, drinking, and other habits; strongly held religious and other beliefs; friendships and blood or marital ties with other members of the Relationship Web.

This kind of personal information, which is what friends usually know about each other, eventually emerges in most good relationships. It enables people to understand what they have in common and to avoid offending one another. It provides a framework for shared ideas, values, hopes, and ambitions. It generates empathy. Most of this information isn't public and thus will be revealed by the individual, more quickly by some than others. Relationships are built on shared experiences and shared confidences, so sooner or later most people who work together over time come to know this (and perhaps even more personal) information about one another.

Until you are very familiar with someone, you will need a system for keeping track of all this data. Index cards or a more formal record-keeping system, or computer files or specialized software, can help. Even if someone you're getting to know realizes that you "remember" the name of her son only because you wrote it down, she will still appreciate your effort and professionalism.

You cannot—and should not attempt to—pry personal information from a business associate. You can, however, offer *appropriate* information about yourself and, more importantly, listen to the other person. Knowing someone and letting him know you is essential to every good relationship. It's a process that can take place during every contact. Nonetheless, knowing as much as you can—given the cost of developing the information in light of the importance of the stakeholder—*before* you make contact will set you apart from the vast majority of people who will approach that person this year. Companies searching for acquisition candidates, marketers in direct mail, and businesses moving into foreign markets do huge amounts of research and planning to maximize their chances of success. Why not give yourself the same advantage in every prospective relationship?

FROM THE RAM PLAYBOOK

To populate your Relationship Web, you must constantly expose yourself to the possibility of new relationships. That constant exposure occurs only when you place yourself in situations where you'll meet new people.

We own and oversee Hardaway's Firehouse Four, a restaurant on Brickell Avenue in downtown Miami. People ask us all the time why we invested in a restaurant/nightclub. It's a tough and fickle business with many hassles and small margins. We went into the business mainly to have a venue for meeting people, and it has succeeded beyond our wildest expectations.

In the two years that we've owned the restaurant, we've met more people in more walks of life than we could have in 10 years of milling around town: CEOs, entrepreneurs, bankers, attorneys, politicians, judges, city managers, celebrities, entertainers, sports figures, and just downright nice people. Since we sold SCG, the Firehouse has been the main "feeder" of our Relationship Web.

If you open a restaurant or a store—or join an organization—to launch a cultivation effort, be sure to do two things: First, choose a venue that will expose you to a range of potential stakeholders. We chose a restaurant because our goal was to meet the broadest possible array of people in our city. Your cultivation goals might be more focused, but don't limit yourself to a professional or industry association (although it's good to join a couple). Also consider a civic group such as Kiwanis or the Chamber of Commerce. Second, become active in the endeavor, whatever it is. It's not enough to read the newsletter and show up at meetings. Get involved in committees and take a leadership role in some effort. Find a task that no one wants to do, and then do it well and move on to other positions in the group. That way you don't just meet people, you get to know them.

DO WE HAVE CONTACT?

If business is a contact sport, here's where the game begins. Information about a company or a person cannot, in itself, create a relationship. You must establish and then maintain contact with that person. An initial contact can range from a chance encounter with someone you've never thought of as being on your Relationship Web to a day-long meeting for which you've spent weeks in preparation. In between lay unexpected encounters with people you have researched, as well as prearranged meetings with someone on your list.

Whenever possible, try to meet a potential stakeholder by introduction through a mutual acquaintance. That sounds obvious, but in our experience few people take full advantage of this tactic. Many underestimate its power. Others mistakenly think that they "don't know anyone." (If that were true, a strong dose of RAM would be the best remedy.) If you've done your homework and believe that you have a potential win for the person you're pursuing, search your entire Relationship Web—and the webs of those on your web—for someone who can introduce you. Then ask him to do so. Tell the mutual acquaintance your purpose—"I'd like to approach your friend Jerry, and here's why." This acquaintance might also be able to help you identify wins for "Jerry." Bring your acquaintance into the process, if you can. Ask him if you should meet in person or whether it would be better to use his name in a letter or on the phone. When someone calls one of us and says, "So-and-so suggested that I give you a call," we take the call. An in-person introduction at a social gathering, at a business function, or over drinks or lunch makes sense if there's high potential for mutual interest.

Enough books and articles have been written on networking that we don't have to dwell on it here. Networking can help you cultivate your Relationship Web and make contact, but you have to do it right. A lot of networking has been done to build business card collections rather than relationships. It's often done without a strategy, research, or planning, and it tends to take a limited or one-sided view of potential wins. Trading business cards won't hurt anybody. But it's wasteful to take the trouble to make contact with someone when all you have is "a handful of nothing and a mouthful of 'much obliged'" (as they say down South).

RAM involves networking with strategic intent and a balanced view of the potential wins. Most networking produces leads rather than introductions. That's the mind-set, so that's the result. A lead isn't worthless; it's just *worth less* than a solid introduction to a carefully selected potential stakeholder.

WARM CALLS VERSUS COLD CALLS

Cold calls have a bad reputation. They're hard to make and they're usually a low-percentage play. What's more, today's automated answering systems, plus the pace of everyone's workday, makes cold calls more difficult than ever—particularly to well-insulated decision-makers.

A well-crafted letter or an intriguing e-mail can warm up a cold call. The volume of mail and e-mail out there today works against this, too, so the more personal, targeted, and compelling you can make your message, the better chance you'll have. In our experience, a letter sent by FedEx never fails to get attention. No one (as of this writing) has refused our follow-up phone call after we've introduced ourselves via a FedEx letter. Expensive? You bet, but worth it if you must get through to a potential stakeholder.

When you use the phone, building relationships with gatekeepers helps the cause. If they want to know the nature of your call, share whatever information you think might make them stakeholders in your effort to get through. After a few rounds of courteous but persistent phone calls, an assistant usually—out of sympathy or exhaustion—will ask the elusive executive to take your call, especially if you leaven the situation with humor.

If you're clever, try clever ways of getting through. An advertising firm we know of sent media buyers golf balls embossed with "Kincaid Advertising is on the ball." This demonstrated creativity in a creative business. Don't get cute if you are not in a business that likes cute (money management springs to mind), but think beyond the standard tactics. With good research on the people you're approaching, you should be able to devise a personally appealing opening move.

Regardless of how you achieve it, the initial contact will probably offer little opportunity for building a relationship. If a connection is to develop, at least one party must begin to work at it. This happens through a series of contacts, or what we call "touches." A touch can be a letter, note, e-mail, phone call, meeting, or luncheon.

Before the initial contact, you must—repeat, must—determine a reason for a follow-up touch. The reason for the follow-up could change during the initial contact, but you need to open a path to the next contact. Then, for each subsequent contact, have a couple of good reasons for following up. We define a successful contact at this early stage as one that lays the groundwork for subsequent contacts.

When the reason for the next contact has been established, at least in your own mind, everything depends on follow-through. If you absolutely cannot think of a reason to follow up, at least call or e-mail the person to thank him for his time or to say that it was good to meet him. However, more effective follow-up would entail this:

- Delivering on a promise that you made during the initial contact, for example, to supply information about your company or the name of someone who could somehow help the person

- Mailing a clipping of an article that might be of interest

- E-mailing a short note along with the address (and hyperlink) to a Web site that the person might not have seen

- Putting the person on the mailing list for your quarterly newsletter "for clients and friends of _____ (Your) Company"

- Extending an invitation to cocktails, lunch, or an event that you know the person would find interesting

Does this strike you as insincere or Machiavellian? It's not. Rather, it's the way business contacts are formed. Remember, you've taken the trouble to learn about this person and his organization. Moreover, you are committed to building either a win-win relationship with him or none at all. You're not the first one to approach the person in this way—just one among several. Unless you've presented yourself as something you're not (such as a would-be biographer or marriage material), the stakeholder understands that you have a business motive in pursuing him. That's not going to upset anyone.

GETTING CONNECTED

Making contact gets you into the game. You've gotten on the stakeholder's screen by letting him know he's on yours. Your "touches" communicate that and keep you in contact. Connection begins with discussions about how you can do business together.

In business, RAM is about business. This Yogi Berra–like statement distinguishes the business from the personal dimensions of RAM. At all stages of relationship development—research, planning, contact, and connection—you're getting to know the stakeholder as a person. But the objectives are business objectives. Therefore, the key tasks are to develop mutual trust and get the desired wins of both parties on the table. Both trust and discussion of wins are essential. One without the other will not create a win-win business relationship.

Throughout the process of connecting, of building trust and discussing wins, both parties set expectations for one another. We recommend setting expectations with the precision of a diamond cutter. When people have precise expectations of the relationship, they know their wins, the other party's wins, and what they have to do by when in order to achieve those wins. Early in the process of connecting, expectations are set at a broad level. What are the most important things to each party, and why? What is each party's biggest problem at the moment? How have things gone over the past few years for each party in terms of finances, growth, and meeting goals?

Don't expect to set expectations precisely on the first few contacts. When a diamond cutter works, he knows the overall shape he's going to create. That shape reflects his perception of the possibilities and flaws in the stone, which he spends time discovering at the outset. He shapes the stone with successive cuts and adjusts his original vision as necessary, always remembering that striking too hard or along the wrong vector will ruin the stone. Shaping expectations starts with defining the outlines of the deal or relationship. In successive contacts, you learn more about the possibilities for mutual wins and build trust along the way. With some people, extreme care must be exercised or the relationship will be jeopardized. An amateurish assumption or unrealistic expectation can shatter trust and put you farther back than square one.

Ultimately, expectations must be clearly understood by both parties. Contracts are the most common tool for this, but contracts cannot take the place of trust, nor can they fix a deal, let alone a relationship, that was flawed from the beginning. Suing to enforce a contract does provide recourse—expensive, time-consuming recourse—so it's best to look at a contract as a way of clarifying expectations and formalizing the commitment. Contracts do provide insurance, but, as with most insurance, you don't want to have to use it.

FROM THE RAM PLAYBOOK

In our hiring process at SCG, we set employee expectations by detailing the company culture, job content, travel requirements, and other aspects of the position. We first administered a test that determined whether the candidate possessed the analytical skills to do the job. If the candidate passed the test, our job was to set the expectations precisely and see if the person was a cultural fit.

We had a list of five expectations: First, people had to work as a team. We didn't want a "star system" at our company, so we built a team environment. Second, heavy travel was part of the job; third, so were overtime and long hours. We tried to be sensitive on these issues, but they were realities. Fourth, everyone was always on a learning curve. There was no way to learn the job and then cruise. Fifth, we had certain salary and advancement parameters.

We explained these expectations, asked probing questions, and observed the candidate's reactions. What problems would heavy travel create for you? When have you succeeded as a team member, and when did you succeed solely on your own? What are your advancement expectations? And so on. If someone said, "Well, my last job had 60 percent travel, and my spouse found it really difficult," we told them that the position wasn't right. Taking time and trouble up front to set expectations precisely saved us untold amounts of time and trouble down the road.

Gauging the pace of the relationship—the number of "touches" to employ as you build the connection and the precision of the discussions about wins—represents a skill. Like all skills, this is learned through practice. We do have ideas and guidelines on maintaining relationships, which we'll share in Principle #10, "Get Rolling and Maintain Momentum."

When the research is done, the contact is made, and a connection is forming, then the relationship has begun. At this point, a successful RAM strategy depends on avoiding relationship killers, which we cover in Principle #8. It also depends on developing wins for both parties, which we cover in the next principle.

- Successful people view working to develop relationships as an essential aspect of business life. They understand the "business agenda," and so do the people they approach. If friendships develop, that's wonderful, but if the relationship remains at a business level, that's fine, too.

- Preparation—researching a potential stakeholder and planning an approach to the initial contact and to follow-up contacts—dramatically increases the chances of igniting a relationship.

- If an introduction through a mutual acquaintance isn't possible, a letter sent by mail, e-mail, or FedEx can warm up a cold call. Pleasant persistence pays off when pursuing a potentially worthwhile stakeholder.

- An initial contact offers scant opportunity for building a relationship. Use early contacts to gather more information about the stakeholder, while laying the groundwork for subsequent contacts.

- Connection begins with more focused discussions of how you can help one another toward mutual wins. This should begin early in the process, at least on a broad level. You want to set expectations with the precision of a diamond cutter, which could require time and patience.

PRINCIPLE #5:

MOVE INTO THE WIN-WIN ZONE

Magic Johnson believed that if he helped everyone around him get what they wanted out of the
game, then winning would always follow. And so
would his own rewards, in their own time and of
their own accord.

—*From* The Winner Within, *by Pat Riley, coach,
Miami Heat*

What an attitude for a new player to bring to professional basketball. Many guys would be thinking at that moment, "I'm gonna be a star. Get out the record books." Many others would entertain doubts about whether they would really make in pro ball. But Earvin "Magic" Johnson took a different approach, one that was so win-win that this passage quoted from Pat Riley's book jumped off the page at us. And that approach worked. Magic Johnson went on to become a star among stars in the Lakers dynasty of the 1980s, beloved by fans, teammates, and even opponents.

Take a moment, if you would, to consider your attitude toward your career or business venture. Also consider your approach toward the key people you interact with day to day.

You probably want to do a great job. You probably want to delight your boss, satisfy your customers, and outdo your competitors. Most people want to excel professionally. However, it's not the desire to excel but the way we define excellence that determines our approach to business and the relationships we create. When you're defining excellence, it's natural to focus on *your* plans, *your* performance, and *your* wins. The fallacy of central position dictates that most of us will do exactly that. The fallacy of central position holds that each human being sees himself as the center of the universe and perceives the world from that position. That fallacy drives each of us to focus instinctively on *our* wins.

This is why Magic Johnson's approach struck his coach, and us, as noteworthy. Notice that Johnson is by no means disinterested in his wins. He wants to be on a winning team, and he wants the rewards that go with that. He just happens to believe that those things will come to him if he helps everyone around him to achieve their wins. That attitude goes beyond saying, "If the team wins, I win." That's a laudable thought, but it's not specific enough. Johnson's approach, as expressed by Riley, says hypothetically, "If Kareem Abdul Jabar wants to dunk, I'll get him the ball when he's under the basket. If James Worthy likes to shoot from the top of the key, I'll set picks so that he can do that." And so on.

Virtually every person you want to do business with wants wins of some kind. Find out what those wins are and what role you can play in creating them, and you're on your way to a fruitful relationship. Now we're assuming that you've done the work up to this point. You've identified and started building connections with stakeholders, and you have some idea of the wins that they might be able to help you achieve. To get those wins, though, you're going to have to help those stakeholders achieve *their* wins. This principle details how do to that.

WAYS TO FIND WINS

Pursuing win-centric relationships differs sharply from waiting for wins to happen. It also differs from assuming that the other party is winning simply by doing business with you. You can't say, "If employees are working for us, if customers are buying from us, and if shareholders are investing in us, they must be happy." Stakeholders don't always tell you when they're unhappy. In fact, most don't. Instead, they make other plans and then pull up stakes. Moreover, even happy stakeholders could no doubt be happier (remember how our headhunter in Principle #4, "Transform Contacts into Connections," works?). If you don't make them happier, someone else will. Therefore, the process of finding and delivering wins never stops.

BEYOND THE BUCKS

As noted earlier, money is always a factor in business, but nonmonetary wins are also important. Although they might be secondary to money, they're a close second. At times and to certain stakeholders, they are even more important. In RAM strategy, they are always critical because a relationship—in fact, the whole experience of doing business with one set of people versus another set—provides many nonmonetary wins. Because RAM focuses on relationships, it is a way of doing business that goes beyond purely financial concerns.

Consider the power of nonmonetary wins among employees. It is well known that good pay is necessary, but not sufficient, to motivate employees. Management scientist Edward Deming went so far as to say that pay is not a motivator. We believe that money is a motivator—nobody works for free—but Deming's point supports the philosophy of RAM. Money cannot in itself create good employee relationships. People want to feel good about the way they earn their money. They want challenging work, recognition, bosses they respect, and a safe and attractive workplace. More than ever, employees also seek benefits beyond healthcare insurance and a retirement plan, including "lifestyle benefits" such as onsite daycare and fitness facilities.

One could argue that some nonmonetary wins are really monetary. For example, onsite day care and fitness facilities save the employee from paying market rates for these services and the costs of traveling to them. Even so, these wins go beyond the employees' monetary compensation.

Nonmonetary wins can be equally important to customers. In a free-market economy, competitive forces drive the price-quality equation to similar levels from company to company. At a given price, the difference in quality between a GM car and a Ford, or between a Mercedes and BMW, model for model, is negligible. Yet a host of other wins surround the purchase of an automobile. Car manufacturers are well aware of these wins and do their best to cast their products as purchases that will deliver them. The wins largely center on experiencing feelings of status, thrift, safety, and power and on projecting a certain image. Similar wins surround most other consumer products. The better you know your customer—or any stakeholder—the more of these "psychological" wins you can deliver.

These wins are not always the ones you would expect. In the 1950s, a cake-mix company learned this when sales fell after they added dehydrated eggs to their mixes. Previously, an egg and milk had to be added, but the new formulation required adding only the milk. The fall-off in sales stunned the manufacturer, who had been certain that the convenience of having the egg already in the mix would be a win for busy bakers. They would only have to stir in the milk and bake. However, research conducted after the sales drop-off revealed that the home cooks preferred adding their own egg. Why? Adding the egg made them feel as if they were making the cake from scratch and doing something wholesome for their families.

If this seems like ancient history, consider a more recent example. On March 7, 2001, a front-page article in *The Wall Street Journal* on Hamburger Helper said: "The food industry, obsessed for years with making products ever readier to eat, has had a revelation: Americans want to do a bit, but just a bit, of actual cooking." The article went on to note that although most convenience foods could be cooked in a microwave oven, "the microwave chef is left with little sense of accomplishment."

Hamburger Helper delivers the win of a fast meal *and* the win of feeling that you've prepared it yourself. General Mills vice president Bob Waldron compared his product favorably to frozen pizza for which the home cook "really didn't do much. With Helper … you're stirring. You're browning. You're doing enough." The article also reported that the dried onions that come packed with Philly Cheesesteak Hamburger Helper "give the consumer a heightened sense of involvement in the cooking process." Just like that little old egg did in the mid-twentieth century.

A whole lot of things in this world change, but human nature stays the same. Affiliation, involvement, recognition, accomplishment and all the other emotions and psychological forces at work within stakeholders affect their relationships, including their business relationships—even their relationships with cake mixes and Hamburger Helper.

The challenge in executing RAM strategy is to create as many wins as you can for the people you do business with. Fortunately, it's much easier to find wins, even nonmonetary wins, than the complexities of the food industry might lead you to believe. Two fundamental tools—

spoking out and asking openly—coupled with your knowledge of business and the stakeholder, will help you unearth wins.

SPOKING OUT

Putting yourself in the other guy's shoes amounts to common sense. But like so much common sense, it's easier to ignore than to practice. Spoking out—moving along a "spoke" in the Relationship Web and assuming a stakeholder's position—is a way of seeing a transaction or relationship from the other party's point of view and, from that viewpoint, searching for wins for that stakeholder.

Because every company and every individual stands at the center of their own Relationship Web, an interesting thing occurs when you put yourself in their position. You shift your viewpoint to the center of *their* Relationship Web. This shift is valuable for several reasons:

- First, you realize that you are not the center of their universe. They are the center of their universe. From their point of view, you might hold a much different position in the scheme of things than you thought. (If nothing else, this exercise helps you cope with the fallacy of central position.)

- Second, you can more effectively consider other relationships in the stakeholder's business life and, when relevant, personal life. This can help you understand the pressures and opportunities that they face.

- Third, you can more clearly see ways in which you could lose. Other parties in your stakeholder's Relationship Web might offer him wins that you wouldn't see or couldn't provide.

- Fourth, and most important, you can better envision ways of providing wins for that stakeholder. From the other party's point of view, you can better understand the goals, success factors, and risks that they face and envision ways to craft wins based on them.

Spoking out must be undertaken on the basis of solid information and with empathy and imagination.

Information about stakeholders is gold. The more you know about the plans, operations, finances, and Relationship Webs of your stakeholders, the more wins you'll be able to find for them. Of course, businesspeople have long known that information is power, yet traditionally they've used information to exploit a situation for their own benefit. In contrast, RAM maximizes mutual benefits. There is, however, a self-protective aspect to developing information. Realistically, RAM does not aim to provide wins far beyond those necessary to keep a stakeholder productively engaged, any more than it aims to provide wins far below necessity. The wins must be balanced. Information enables you to craft the stakeholder's wins in proportion to your wins. It helps you steer toward a balanced point in the win-win zone.

Empathy—the capacity for seeing or experiencing another's situation from his perspective—lets you grasp the emotional dimensions of a business situation. When you spoke out, try to gauge how the stakeholder feels. If you provide a win and the stakeholder doesn't feel that it is a win, what have you accomplished? If you think that a deal is win-win but the other party sees it as lose-win, where is the relationship headed? Thus, the task is not only to craft wins, but to craft them so that all parties feel like winners. When you spoke out to a stakeholder's position, do it with empathy, to capture the emotional dimension. Consider the history of the relationship and the personalities and egos involved.

In spoking out, information and empathy work together to give you a fix on the feelings as well as the facts. Then it's time to bring the imagination into play. Imagination enables you to create wins rather than just divvy up the obvious ones. Most people stop far too soon in their search for wins. Bringing imagination into spoking out enables you to search more deeply and to consider wins that wouldn't otherwise occur to you.

We offer the following questions as prompts and thought-starters for spoking out:

1. What is important to this stakeholder besides money?

2. What are the "gimmes" here, the no-brainers? Then what's left?

3. What's the stakeholder's bottom line? What might enable her to change that bottom line?

4. What are the stakeholder's goals? Who do I know who could help her achieve them?

5. What are the stakeholder's key success factors? Does she have them in place? If not, how can I help?

6. What risks does this shareholder face that I (or someone I know) can mitigate?

7. What resources does this stakeholder lack that I (or someone I know) could provide?

8. How can I reduce the stakeholder's costs at no cost to me? How can I reduce her costs by spending a fraction of those costs so that we can share the savings?

9. What business practices—such as bundling, unbundling, adding frills or going no-frills, or rescheduling—might apply here?

10. How can I make it easier for this stakeholder to do business with me?

11. Has this stakeholder had any positive or negative relationship experiences in the past?

12. What personal wins could I provide for this individual?

Notice that most of these are open-ended questions, which can't be answered yes or no. Open-ended questions are more thought-provoking than close-ended ones, which can be answered yes or no. We present this list mainly to encourage you to develop your own questions, although most of them can be applied across stakeholder groups. For instance, questions about reducing costs and making it easier to do business apply not just to customers and suppliers, but to investors as well. Cost reduction and convenience are why many publicly held companies have systems that allow all investors, not just employees, to buy stock directly from the company.

Almost everyone has an array of benefits that they could derive from a given business relationship. Spoking out can help you identify these wins like no other tactic. Although the more information you have to go on, the better, you can use this technique even before you meet the potential stakeholder. When you use it beforehand, you'll ask better questions about that person's wins because you will have thought things through from his point of view.

One other thing about spoking out: When you survey the Relationship Web from someone else's point of view, you might well see that a potential stakeholder of that person is someone you have a relationship with and can introduce or influence in his favor. That's a great win to be able to offer, but one that might not come up for quite a while unless you actively seek it in this way.

IF YOU WANT TO KNOW, JUST ASK

Several years ago, the investment firm PaineWebber ran a television campaign in which two co-workers, a man and a woman, were talking about the woman's early retirement. The man envied her and wondered how her financial advisers knew that early retirement had been her goal. The woman looked at the man pointedly and said, "They asked." PaineWebber ran a number of ads with the same punch line, and critical and public response showed the campaign to be quite effective.

Asking stakeholders about the wins they would like to achieve is simple and direct. Though it is more easily done with people you know well, we recommend asking about wins early in a business relationship. In some situations, you can even bring up the subject of wins the first time you meet the person. The wording goes something like this:

"Here are the wins I would like to achieve, provided that we can do business together and get a relationship going. And here are some of the wins that I believe you would get out of the relationship. What I would like to do is learn more about your potential wins and maybe modify my own. How does this sound to you?"

Opening a discussion or meeting in this manner sets a businesslike tone while setting up an agenda aimed at defining and finding mutual wins. It's a way of saying, "Let's see if you and I can help each other out by doing business." This sort of opening enables each party to put forth ideas regarding their goals in a deal or relationship, and to modify or withdraw those ideas, depending on the other party's response. Each party also gets to hear the other's ideas in an atmosphere of exploration. In an exploratory discussion, people can define the parameters of a deal or a budding relationship without prematurely committing themselves to anything.

Many people make the mistake of believing that everything comes down to money, so they don't even ask about other wins. Yes, employees want higher salaries, customers want lower prices, and investors want increasing returns. However, a company can deliver many other potential wins to stakeholders. As we've noted, many of these wins are nonmonetary. Nonmonetary wins also can lead to monetary wins. For instance, financial folklore says that a young man once approached J.P. Morgan for a loan. The legendary financier refused to extend the loan, but instead he invited the man to accompany him on a stroll around the perimeter of the New York Stock Exchange. Observers saw the young man walking and chatting with Morgan and were impressed, to say the least. The would-be borrower received an immediate win—pride of association with J.P. Morgan—and a financial win later, when he approached potential lenders and investors who had seen him with Morgan from the floor of the exchange.

It can be difficult to ask about nonmonetary wins such as ego grat-ification, bragging rights, pride of association, and issues of status. Despite what some television shows depict, not everyone enjoys talking about their "feelings." However, certain stakeholders, such as customers, can be approached about these matters. For example, General Mills and most other large packaged-goods companies hold focus groups where people describe the experiences, emotions, and associations they have when using a product. With some stakeholders, though, rather than ask about emotionally based wins, it's best to present the win as one you would both naturally want—"You'll look good to your boss, and I'll look good to mine"—and watch for the response.

FROM THE RAM PLAYBOOK

Here's a great question to ask a potential stakeholder when you want to discover his wins: *What are your ambitions for your business?* (Or, depending on the stakeholder, for your career, community, publication, charitable foundation, or whatever applies.)

In response, we've heard things like, "To triple the size of this operation in three years," and "To see my competitors go bankrupt," and (too often) "Gee, I really don't know." But we've found that almost any answer to that question will open a path for a deeper discussion of wins.

Here's why the question works so well: First, it's open-ended and, therefore, more thought-provoking than a yes-or-no question. Second, you're assuming that they have ambitions, and that's flattering. You think of them as play-ers. Third, you're indicating that you care about their longer-term situation. You're inviting them to join you in thinking beyond the immediate transaction. Finally, the other party will often share a deeply desired win, or least start thinking about one. Then you can start helping the stakeholder chart a course toward that big win.

Of course, if the stakeholder is your employee and her most fervent ambition is to get out of your company by the end of the month, you won't get a straight answer. In general, though, whatever you hear will be revealing.

Doing business in the context of RAM strategy depends on a continual search for wins. It's the process of asking yourself about your wins, asking the other party about its wins, and, if possible, asking several people on the other side of the deal about potential wins. Aside from asking about wins, ask about how the other party does business. How does the company make its product? Where do the materials come from? What's the sales process?

In Principle #1, "See Relationships as Valuable Assets," we mentioned that we developed an agreement with a software vendor: We would give the vendor the win of constructing customized demos for its salespeople at our own expense, and the vendor would give us the win of introducing us to its clients and prospects. But we didn't figure out the win we could offer in our first conversation, which was with the president of the firm. We tumbled to the idea of offering to construct the demos only after the president introduced us to the sales manager. In the course of the conversation with the sales manager, we asked how the company went about selling, and he mentioned that they were using standard demos with Acme Company and widgets and so on. It was then that we asked, "What if your salespeople could demonstrate their software with the prospects information and customized reports?" The sales manager saw the value right away. It was a much better and more concrete win than if we could offer only to share our sales leads in return for theirs.

LIVING IN THE ZONE

Our restaurant, Hardaway's Firehouse Four, has been a challenging environment in which to practice RAM strategy. It's a full-service restaurant serving lunch and dinner in a downtown location. It's also a nightclub, providing entertainment in one section. When we started, we had no experience in the restaurant business, and we've found it to be as complex as any other business. A restaurant provides the general public with something of a luxury, so its success partially depends on fad and fashion, and Miami is a trendy town. That's a difficult situation in which to forge long-term relationships.

Yet we've applied RAM strategy to the restaurant and continue to do so. Our reasoning on the basic success factors goes like this: The location of the restaurant is a given. We can't move the firehouse. (Yes, it used to be an actual firehouse.) Fortunately, it's a good location, downtown on Brickell Avenue near residential complexes, with more apartments under construction as of this writing. When fully occupied, the new buildings will house an additional 5,000 people or so—all of whom must eat every day of their lives. The other success factors—the food, service, and ambiance—are all as good as we and our management team and staff can make them, and we all work to improve continually in those areas.

So after the basic success factors are nailed down, where does RAM apply in this business? Almost everywhere.

COURTING CUSTOMERS

In applying RAM strategy, we thought long and hard about building relationships with customers. Beyond delivering a good value and an enjoyable dining experience, restaurants try various tools for building customer relationships. A standard one involves inviting diners to drop their business cards into a fish bowl for a prize drawing, and then compiling mailing lists for coupons and notices about events and special menus.

We felt that we needed a higher-powered approach, for one reason: economics. A fantastically loyal dinner patron, coming in twice a week, year-in and year-out, will spend maybe $50 a meal with a drink and wine. That totals $100 a week or $5,000 a year. These are wonderful customers, and we have our share of them. But as a proportion of all customers, they amount to one in several hundred. Most repeat diners (as opposed to happy-hour patrons) come in much less frequently. People who dine out regularly like to move around. They enjoy trying different places, experiencing new tastes and atmospheres. They come back, but they dine elsewhere, too. When it comes to most customers, you're going to get only a certain share of wallet.

So after doing everything we could to deliver on the food, service, and ambiance, we realized that we still needed to build our customer traffic and revenue. What other wins could we provide customers? What would be the wins for us? The answers were not as simple as we thought.

First, we did start a happy hour, and thanks to our excellent staff, our downtown location, and our widespread Relationship Web, it is not only well-attended, but it was also voted Best Happy Hour in South Florida (twice in its three-year existence) on CitySearch.

Second, perhaps because of the success of the happy hour, we began to think about building relationships with *groups* of customers as well as with individual customers. That thought led us to review our experiences at SCG, which had been a business-to-business enterprise but still might hold some valuable lessons. That's when a light bulb lit up. Most companies need a place where they can entertain people, host events, hold holiday parties, and hang out at happy hour. Many companies need to outsource their corporate catering. With our location and experience, we decided to make Firehouse Four that place for as many companies as we could. We hired a caterer, got the word out, and leveraged and built relationships.

For instance, a major cruise line entertains travel agents, so we asked the company to try the Firehouse for some of that entertaining. When they came in, we worked as hard as we could to deliver wins and to make the person who chose our restaurant look like a winner. The RAM process works here, just like it does in other industries. There is a living, breathing person who decides where a company does its entertaining, and the task is to build a relationship with that person, learn their wins, and then deliver. And it's working. Corporate catering—where a single relationship brings in a significant multiple of the annual revenue on one loyal patron—is the fastest-growing segment of our restaurant.

Here's the moral of the story: When you're doing everything right—as we were in food, service, and ambiance—but are still short of your goals, take a step back and look at the environment and the economics. Who has a need out there? Which wins could you deliver? Where can you leverage relationships? How might you take a wholesale, rather than retail, approach to building relationships? Where's the biggest bang for the buck? How can you reprioritize your efforts so that you keep current relationships while building new ones?

VIVA LOS VENDORS

In the restaurant business, you basically buy from food suppliers and soft drink, beer, wine, and liquor distributors. Most of them—particularly the beer, wine, and liquor distributors—have promotional budgets. They want a relationship with us, and we want a relationship with them, so making contacts and maintaining connections is part of the daily routine. Nevertheless, you need creativity to develop wins for suppliers because their promotional budgets are not unlimited. They don't throw money at you. So, we've experimented with ways of getting our vendors involved in some of our efforts to attract people to the restaurant—things such as jazz night on Wednesdays, Latin night on Thursdays, and a disk jockey on Fridays.

Our greatest success in this area has been the grand opening of Hardaway's Firehouse Four, when we changed the name of the restaurant to reflect the involvement of Tim Hardaway, star point guard with the Miami Heat. Our chief desired win was to host a great event while keeping our costs down. The vendors' main desired win was to promote their brands. And both of us wanted the win of maximum media exposure. We laid all of this out for our distributors, and, sure enough, a couple of them pitched in by providing appetizers and drinks. A liquor supplier provided service people to assist our staff. We, in turn, banged the drum to bring in television and press coverage. As we announced Tim coming on board, the TV cameras caught the liquor company's banner in the background, and 500 influential people got to sample the distributor's products. It was a win-win for all concerned.

DON'T FIGHT CITY HALL

It's fairly easy for a business to get into an adversarial relationship with the local government. The city has taxes, building and health codes, zoning laws, traffic control and noise abatement issues, plus crime to stop and fires to put out (literally). Any or all of these can impact any business, and too many businesspeople view the city as some kind of enemy. For its part, the city could well view a business as one more problem that it doesn't need.

Knowing all this, we took a highly proactive approach to developing a win-win relationship with key people in the city government. We could not afford to do otherwise because, first, we see no point in having *any* adversarial relationships, and second, we lease the firehouse and the property under it from the city of Miami. We and the city are, in a very real sense, strategic partners in the enterprise. Therefore, early on we met with the asset manager, the city manager, and the mayor, and shared our philosophy with them. Because we were in partnership, we could be entirely up front about developing mutual wins. If we succeeded, the city succeeded; if we failed, the city failed in this endeavor. Thus, whenever the city helped the restaurant win, the city helped itself win. (Before we took over and renovated it, the restaurant had stood vacant for a year and a half. The previous establishment had failed, and the property had been seized by the city for back taxes.)

Our target wins included having some city meetings and events held at the Firehouse; landing introductions to various corporate, charitable, and community organizations; and receiving assistance if we needed it with aspects of the business, which, again, they had leased to us. The city managers and professionals were open to these ideas and have been extremely helpful. One recent Friday night at 5:00, a repair crew from the county began working on the sewers in front of the restaurant. This meant blocking the road, cranking an air compressor up to 200 decibels, and filling the atmosphere with sewer gas—on our biggest night of the week. It would have killed our business for that evening and cost us thousands of dollars. We called the city manager, and even though it was the county and not the city doing the work, she drove over, learned what was going on, found out who to talk to at the county, and called them. In 15 minutes, the repair crew had packed up and left. They returned to do the job on Sunday, when we're closed.

Without a doubt, our relationship with the city has helped us tremendously. It's a genuine asset, for both parties. As a matter of fact, as of this writing we're now in the process of working up a RAM seminar for the city's asset manager and her 30 employees.

HOOP DREAMS

When we were introduced to Tim Hardaway, we mentioned to him that we are businessmen who make investments in what we believe will be interesting, profitable ventures. Note that Tom Richardson mentioned this the very first time we met Tim, who casually asked us to keep him in mind if something came up. We agreed to do that. Moreover, we told him that we would inform him only about deals that we were putting money into ourselves.

We kept in contact, and when the opportunity to invest in Horizon Bank came up, we told Tim about it and he bought some shares. This established a business relationship between us and provided mutual wins. The wins occurred at a monetary level *and* at the nonmonetary level in terms of building trust, getting to know one another, and being invested together in the greater Miami community.

The notion of a celebrity somehow being connected with Firehouse Four had occurred to us from time to time. Like most major cities, Miami has many good restaurants, and an endorsement by one of the city's popular athletes can help an establishment distinguish itself from others. One day Tim stopped by, and in the course of a conversation, Tom asked him, "What would you think about the idea of Hardaway's Firehouse Four?" Tim liked the general concept, and we worked out a deal to make the idea a reality.

We all won financially. As restaurateurs, we won by receiving more publicity than we dreamed possible, from the launch party through coverage of Hardaway's Firehouse Four by ESPN and other sports shows, to the continuing use of the restaurant as a site for interviews. Tim won by forming another connection to the community, keeping his name before the Miami public year-round in another venue, and having a familiar, convenient restaurant to go to with friends and family.

All of these good things began with an introduction, followed up by contact and a steady search for mutual wins.

LOOKING FOR W'S

Still relatively new to the restaurant business, we're continuing to build our Relationship Web in this area and are always seeking wins for ourselves and others. We're currently developing relationships with promoters, who in Miami can make the difference between a successful place and a wildly successful place. They are in very high demand, which makes figuring out their wins—aside from their fee and the opportunity to score another success—challenging.

We're also creating a network of "unofficial promoters" around town. We've distributed cards to taxi drivers with their names on them. When a fare asks the cabby for the name of a good restaurant, he gives her the card and we give the cabby Firehouse Dollars good for free food and drinks. We've recently extended this program to concierges at the downtown hotels.

We cooperate with our competitors—other full-service restaurants in the vicinity—by sharing staples such as beer, wine, or a case of lettuce or bag of potatoes when one of us runs short. When we started out in the business, we approached competitors with the idea of creating a purchasing consortium to increase our leverage with suppliers. We couldn't get them interested, though, due to deeply ingrained purchasing habits and their belief that they could get better deals by buying independently.

That's a bit about how we used RAM to develop wins in the restaurant business. In the next two chapters, we'll explore ways of getting to know your stakeholders as people and of building bonds of trust between you and them.

- As is the case when making contacts and connections, you cannot wait for wins to develop. You have to proactively develop them.

- The financial wins in a business relationship are always important, but nonmonetary wins can be equally important—and sometimes even more important.

- Nonmonetary wins take a variety of forms, ranging from the practical, such as flex-time for employees, to the emotional, such as increased status or a greater sense of affiliation.

- Spoking out—putting yourself in the other party's position and then considering his goals, success factors, and risks—can enable you to find wins that the other party might not even think of.

- Asking directly about the wins that the other party would like to achieve in a deal—and being willing to discuss your target wins—can move the relationship forward.

- When seeking stakeholders, look everywhere in your Relationship Web and beyond, to everyone in the vicinity. You'll be astonished at how many bystanders will become stakeholders if you can make them winners.

PRINCIPLE #6:

GET TO KNOW YOUR STAKEHOLDERS AS PEOPLE

She was a stopper. Chris would do anything necessary to break up a power play, confound a two-on-one, or protect her goalie. She was ferocious. But Chris Bailey's off-ice personality was quite different. She was full of fun and very much the sentimentalist.

—*From* Crashing the Net: The U.S. Women's Olympic Ice Hockey Team and the Road to Gold, *by Mary Turco*

Most of us in business have worked with men or women who keep their "game face" on during the workday but who also, after hours, can kick back, loosen up, and have a few laughs. When someone does that, you might feel as if you're with a different person. On the other hand, not all of these game-face types open up at the end of the day—at least, not the first day you meet them, or even the second or third. Some people need to know you well before they can be themselves in your presence. Others appear to be open books right from the initial contact. Yet those people will surprise you, too. Once you know them better, you might realize that you weren't really seeing the real person at all.

In other words, your stakeholders are human beings, and they possess all the complexities and contradictions that this implies. They might present themselves to you, and relate to you, purely in their roles as stakeholders, but they are actually people first and stakeholders second. That's where Principle #6 comes in. You will build the best relationships by getting to know your stakeholders not only as stakeholders, but as people.

Business relationships that include a personal dimension make doing business more efficient, more effective, and definitely more fun. Imagine a purchasing manager and a supplier at courtside, begging their favorite player to launch a three-pointer, yelling for a foul that the ref refuses to see, and buying each other beers. That's fun, right? Then imagine a phone call between them the following week. This is business. One of them has bad news. The supplier sees a price increase coming, or the purchasing manager needs a rush order. But the problem occurs in a different, more personal context than it otherwise would. In this context, there's greater likelihood that they'll work things out smoothly. Notice that this is the case even without their having become actual friends. Merely sharing a night out at a sporting event brings a personal dimension to the business relationship.

We're not implying that personal considerations should distort or override business considerations. Nor are we saying that you can become friends with every stakeholder. The former would be bad business, and the latter is not realistic. Like players on a professional sports team, businesspeople spend time together, work together, and help one another, not out of kindness or even, necessarily, friendship. They do it out of enlightened self-interest and because they are stakeholders in one another's success. Yet usually, the better people on a team know one another, the more smoothly the team functions. This often occurs naturally as shared goals foster close relationships. It occurs much more frequently if you know how to get to know people.

Those words—know how to get to know people—might seem like an odd turn of a phrase. Doesn't everyone know how to do that? The answer, at least in business, is "No." Some people see their stakeholders only "in role" and can't look beyond the role and see the individuals. Other people prefer a barrier between their business and personal lives, and apply that barrier to the people they meet in business as well as to the work itself. However, the most successful people, from both financial and, we believe, personal standpoints, know how to get to know the people they deal with in business.

BUILDING BONDS

In Spanish, there are two verbs for "to know"—*saber* (*sa-bear*) and *conocer* (*co-no-ser*). *Saber* is to know facts and information. *Conocer* is to know deeply, to experience a person, place, or culture. Personal relationships, bonds between people based on rapport, respect, and trust, lead to good working relationships. They also—and this warrants emphasis—make doing business more fun. Knowing stakeholders as people involves more than acquiring information (*saber*), which, as we saw in Principle #4, "Transform Contacts into Connections," is an essential step in making contact and forming a connection. Creating personal bonds means really knowing someone (*conocer*), and that occurs only when you spend time with him in off-the-job situations. In social situations, you gain a deeper knowledge of someone's personality, character, motivations, and values. That knowledge carries over to the business arena and broadens and deepens the relationship.

The stakeholder gains more knowledge of you as well. This is a two-way street. Relationships are built on *shared* experiences and confidences. We don't mean that you must experience life-changing events together (although that might occur) or share confidences of a deeply personal nature (although that might happen when business associates become close friends). But to know one another as people, you must get beyond talking only about business and beyond knowing one another only in your business roles.

STAGES OF KNOWING

For the purposes of RAM, we've defined four stages to knowing a person in the *conocer* sense of the term:

1. **Awareness of facts and reputation.** The result of research, reading, and listening to others' opinions and experiences of the stakeholder.

2. **Awareness of one another.** The result of the initial meeting, whether through an introduction, a cold call, or a chance meeting.

3. **Knowledge of one another "in role."** The result of repeated contacts or touches in which you gather more information, establish a business relationship, and move into the win-win zone.

4. **Bonding.** The result of interacting socially, exchanging personal information, acting on shared interests, and establishing common ground.

We covered the first three stages in the preceding two principles. Bonding comprises the final step in creating a long-term relationship with openness about goals, success factors, and risks, and with increased opportunities for mutual wins. Bonding involves discovering or creating common ground and then building on that. Common ground could develop around shared interests or experiences: graduating from the same school, rooting for the same sports teams, going to the same happy hour on Friday evening, playing the same golf course, or liking the same books, movies, or music.

The information that enables you to discover or create common ground with a stakeholder is valuable, and a lot of it can be exchanged in the course of a meeting or lunch. That information must be captured. Whether you use a notebook, a laptop, or (as does a colleague of ours in his car after a meeting) a small tape recorder, you have to take note of facts about the person. A stakeholder might mention where he went to school, where his kids go to school, where he plays golf, what he did last weekend, and other bits and pieces that make up the picture of the whole person. People share this information because they want you to know them, but it's impossible to remember it all days or even weeks later. Have a system that will "remember" it for you; if the stakeholder figures out that you kept track of a few facts about him, he'll be flattered and impressed.

The location of the initial contact, and perhaps the next few touches, will probably be a business setting—but not necessarily. Business relationships have started with meetings at a dinner party, on a community project, or at parents' night at school. Wherever the initial contact takes place, the essential step, as noted in Principle #4, is to find reasons for subsequent touches. Those reasons—mailing a magazine article, following up on a promise to supply a name, or extending a social invitation—should reference and build on common interests. To a degree, maintaining contact with a relationship you are cultivating can be viewed almost as a game. How can you stay on that person's screen and keep her on yours? How many legitimate ways are there to stay in touch with this person? Of course, this no longer applies after you have established common ground and a rhythm to the relationship. But cultivating people takes conscious effort and a plan, which is why very few people do a first-rate job of it.

While planning and maintaining contact to establish a bond, be sure to keep frequency, appropriateness, and boundaries in mind.

FREQUENCY

Limit the frequency of your touches to a reasonable number. What's reasonable? That depends on the urgency of the business situation, the roles of the individuals, and the receptiveness of the other party as evidenced by his responses. Touch too frequently, and you'll be labeled a pest. Touch too rarely, and you will fall off the person's screen or miss an opportunity. Or, to put it another way, cultivating a relationship resembles caring for a plant: Water it too little, and it dies. Water it too often, and it dies. On top of this, different plants need different amounts of water to survive. You have to get to know your stakeholders to properly gauge frequency.

There's also a bit of an art to getting the frequency right. For instance, every salesperson has a story about missing a sale despite having a regular contact schedule. Typically, these salespeople touch each prospect at some interval and then one day call and learn that the prospect just bought the item from a competitor. Invariably, the salesperson feels that he did the work of "warming up" the prospect—educating him about the product and making him receptive to a sale—only to have the competitor walk away with the reward. Sometimes they feel betrayed by the prospect.

FROM THE RAM PLAYBOOK

In presenting the principles of RAM to business groups, we've met a couple of people who found themselves in an odd situation. While they were working to build a bond with a stakeholder, the process worked too well. The *stakeholder* cranked the frequency up to uncomfortable levels. "This guy wants me to do something with him twice a week!" one participant told us. "I want a relationship with him, but I've got a family, friends, and a life of my own."

This happens because, as in any profession, there are some needy people in business who don't recognize boundaries or can't gauge the right pace for developing a relationship.

In these (relatively rare) instances, make it clear that you are overcommitted, and then *proactively* invite the person to lunch two or three weeks into the future. By taking the initiative to invite them, you defuse any potential ill feelings while showing an interest in them. If after lunch that person suggests getting together the following week, suggest a time farther out in the future. If they call too frequently, wait a day or so before returning the call.

Over time, most people will join you in establishing a comfortable pace and distance for getting to know one another. It happens through a series of invitations, followed by acceptances or "I can't make it that night" responses.

In the very rare instances when a truly neurotic individual wants a close relationship, we suggest ending all contact. Doctors, social workers, and others in the helping professions are taught to keep a distance—a professional space, if you will—between themselves and their clients. When a client persistently tries to close that distance, he's referred to a colleague or directed out of the practice.

The real problem could be that the touches were not frequent enough to establish real top-of-mind awareness or for the prospect to get to know the salesperson and his company well enough.

It's fairly easy to contact a sales prospect (or any other stakeholder) 12 times a year, once a month, even if you're still only cultivating the relationship, *if* you vary your touches. Few people would object to a quarterly mailing of a newsletter geared to their interests. That leaves eight months. Personal mailings—a handwritten note with a magazine clipping or conference brochure—or e-mails with cool attachments or links could cover four of those months nicely. That leaves four months for telephone contact. Varying the media in this way keeps you in touch without the intrusiveness of frequent phone calls or the boredom of repetitive mailings. If you've ever lost an opportunity with a stakeholder to someone else, maybe you were on the wrong frequency.

The right frequency and forms of contact begin to build a bond between you and the stakeholder, whether or not you get much of a response. The stakeholder gets used to hearing from you. This generates top-of-mind awareness. It also acclimates him to your style. He becomes accustomed to the way you come across, recognizes you as a presence, and, after a while, expects your touches. He probably can't help being flattered on some level by your pursuit, and he might come to admire your pleasant persistence. Eventually, someone such as a sales prospect might feel enough of a bond that, if he were approached with another offer, he would feel the need to ask you to make an offer, too, for comparison or out of fairness.

APPROPRIATENESS

Your touches must be appropriate to their recipients. They must be of interest and in good taste. Recommending that an investor you are cultivating see a movie like *Dumb and Dumber* might not be the best type of touch. Similarly, while many of us get a kick out of e-mailed jokes, not everyone shares the same sense of humor.

We know of a job candidate at a multicompany recruiting event who sat down with the recruiter in an interviewing room. To open the conversation, the recruiter asked, "What did you think of our company brochure?" The candidate said, "Aw, I don't bother reading that marketing hype." Not surprisingly, this did not go over well with the recruiter. We told a friend this story, and he said, "Yeah, but another recruiter might have thought, 'Hey, here's an aggressive, regular guy who speaks his mind.' You never know."

And that's the point: You never know. You never know how someone feels about the company literature or off-color jokes, so it's best to stay within the limits of good taste. Relaxing those limits is often part of bonding with someone and is part of the fun. But if the limits are relaxed from the first contact, where do you go from there? (Don't answer that.) Also, some people never relax those limits, or they relax them very little. They will consider you vulgar and will avoid bonding with you. To an extent, you really must feel your way along to determine the appropriateness of bonding techniques with each individual.

BOUNDARIES

Each of us maintains physical, social, and psychological boundaries that help us maintain our physical, social, and psychological well-being. The accepted boundaries along many dimensions of human interaction have been worked out over centuries. For instance, as you might know, the custom of shaking hands originated with people's desire to show they were not holding a weapon. Today (even in the United States) the vast majority of people are unarmed, yet the custom of the handshake continues.

Now most of us agree that shaking hands does not breach our boundaries. Yet a bad handshake or a sweaty palm might hamper the bonding process. Other people go for the two-handed handshake and even throw in a slap on the back or a hug—and some among us don't care for that. To complicate matters, many customs involving boundaries shift across cultures. Japanese bow rather than shake hands. Entire courses are devoted to the cross-cultural aspects of boundaries to assist people in business and government who will be working in a new culture.

If complicated boundaries surround the simple handshake, imagine the potential for misunderstanding psychological and social boundaries. For instance, the United States fancies itself a classless society, and the vast majority of Americans consider themselves middle class. Yet there are clearly professional, educational, income, and social-class boundaries in this country. The CEOs at many major U.S. companies are called by their first names by everyone, but that doesn't mean they'll meet with any employee who wants their ear.

Research, information gathering, and direct observation will help you chart the boundaries recognized by specific stakeholders. As you get to know them as people, you'll learn even more. Respect those boundaries as you build a relationship, and you'll be welcome. Breach them, and you could kill the relationship (as we discuss in Principle #8, "Banish Relationship Killers").

BONDING AGENTS

Bonding takes place in many situations, including business settings. Yet you'll generally accelerate the process by spending time with a stakeholder off the job (although business travel and industry conferences can encourage the process). Opportunities to create bonds range from having a cup of coffee or a few beers together, to attending sporting events or theatrical performances, to spending an afternoon sailing, skiing, or golfing. Later in the process, inviting the stakeholder and his spouse out to dinner or, later still, to your home, tells the person that you consider him special.

That's the purpose of creating opportunities to bond. By inviting business associates to activities, you tell them that you want to know them better and that you don't see them merely playing a role in your company. As in making contact, your stakeholders and potential stakeholders realize that you have a business agenda. They've heard of business entertaining. But they also know that in most situations in the United States today, these invitations are not obligatory, so there's a personal dimension as well.

Maybe you and the stakeholder won't feel a natural affinity. RAM calls for developing relationships, including personal relationships, in business; yet it recognizes that people have different interests and needs. Friendships cannot be forced. The reasons—the "chemistry"—that cause certain people to hit it off and become personally close are elusive, even to social scientists. So, rather than adopt the goal of "bonding," you should aim to create conditions in which bonding can occur. With a little effort (and realistic objectives), you should be able to find something you enjoy together that will help you get to know one another and build some shared experiences and history.

Although they're somewhat less effective, you can create many bonding opportunities by bringing people together in groups. At SCG, our Christmas parties became extremely popular and attained "don't-miss" status with most of our customers and vendors. Departmental or company picnics, barbecues, anniversary date or sales-success parties, as well as softball or basketball games, charitable work, community projects, or an outing to an amusement park are all worth considering. The truly ambitious take white-water rafting or Outward Bound excursions, which many senior management teams have used to forge bonds among themselves.

In all these bonding situations, exercise sensitivity regarding talk of business. Some people, holding to traditional guidelines, feel that business shouldn't be discussed on social occasions. Today, many people take a looser approach. Like so much in the bonding process, a lot depends on the stakeholder. If you bring up doing business together at an appropriate moment and she shows little interest or steers the conversation the other way, the stakeholder probably prefers to discuss business during business hours or in business settings. On the other hand, if she wants to talk business or if she brings up the subject, then by all means do so. Just be sure to get to know your stakeholders—and give them a chance to know you—as people, and not just in your business roles.

Good relationships take time to develop. Bonding really doesn't occur in a single lunch or round of golf, no matter how well things go. Each bonding opportunity represents another point in a succession of contacts. Make the most of each one, but give the relationship time to develop.

CAN'T-MISS BONDING OPPORTUNITIES

Occasionally, situations arise that offer relationship-building opportunities that you just can't pass up.

YOU'RE INVITED

When stakeholders invite you to lunch, a game, or a company event, grab the opportunity. (If you can't attend, enthusiastically request a rain check.) They might be offended if you refuse. After all, they are signaling that they would like to know you better, or they're returning your hospitality. They deserve their chance to play host and reciprocate. Best of all, you can typically learn more about someone on his turf than on yours.

PASS ON VITAL INFORMATION

When you know something that could help a stakeholder make money, save money, or avoid trouble, tell her, unless you would be violating a confidence. That's a win for her, and she will thank you down the road. Be sensitive to what you should and shouldn't pass along, and never violate a confidence or divulge proprietary information. But be aware that situations do arise in which someone could benefit or (more often, it seems) avoid trouble if that person had all the available facts. If you have those facts, why not share them?

LEND A HAND

Showing a stakeholder he can count on you when he's in trouble will form a close bond quickly. When we offered office space, a telephone, and our copier to colleagues on the client side who were laid off, they knew we saw them as people instead of former stakeholders. Most of them initially wondered why we would call them when they were no longer able to give us business. The fact is, we did care about them, out of enlightened self-interest and because we would want someone to do the same for us if the situation were reversed.

Incidentally, remaining in touch with people after they are no longer in their stakeholder roles in relation to you will build a bond between you. From the business standpoint, they will probably enter that role or a similar one down the road. From the personal standpoint, many friendships begin when people keep in touch after their business relationship ends.

SHARE ADVERSITY

Sharing adversity overlaps with lending a hand. Facing a common threat together or helping someone else survive a threat when you are better positioned builds friendships as well as relationships. For example, when Hurricane Andrew destroyed Burger King's headquarters in 1992 (fish were found on the third floor!), we invited the company to temporarily move its entire IS department into our minuscule offices, and they accepted. Many Burger King people working on our premises in the following days had nothing to do with SCG or our joint projects. But we shared space and equipment, and developed a special bond by surviving Andrew together.

It was also a chance for everyone at SCG to bond with one another. Our staff set up deliveries of food, bottled water, and ice for our stakeholders who lived in the damage zone. Often they would arrive to find demolished houses and the family searching for something to salvage, in the heat and without running water. When we arrived unexpectedly with supplies, the effect was gratifying, to say the least. A co-worker of ours said, "I'll never forget the faces of the children when I pulled those Hershey bars out of the cooler." None of us will forget the experience of going through that together.

FROM THE RAM PLAYBOOK

What if you're not socially outgoing? Can you still get to know stakeholders as people? Although RAM may not turn a shrinking violet into a passion flower, these practices can help a shy person deal with the social dimensions of business.

Research is the secret weapon against social jitters, especially in initial contacts. Good information neutralizes fear in almost any situation. It can give you the confidence to make the first move to get a business associate out of the office. Research also enables you to ask questions, and, as any coach in the art of conversation will tell you, asking questions—rather than talking about yourself—keeps a discussion moving.

Rather than focus on your nervousness or the impression you're making, try to draw out the other person with open-ended questions: Where are you from originally? What do you enjoy doing when you're not working? How has it been for you since you _____ (moved to the area, changed jobs, gave birth to triplets, and so on)? Questions show that you're interested in the other person. Moreover, the answers will point the way toward potential wins. Then when you start discussing ways in which you can help that person achieve those wins, he'll find you downright fascinating.

TAKE FOUL-UPS IN STRIDE

Everybody makes mistakes or hits a rough patch from time to time. When a supplier delivers the wrong order or your bank mistakenly bounces a check, hold on to your frustration and the urge to blame someone. Ask them to address the situation, but work with them toward that end in a problem-solving mode. That puts you and the stakeholder on the same side of the table, tackling the problem together, rather than on opposite sides wrestling one another. Displaying patience with people in these circumstances gives them a win—one which, when your organization screws up, they're not likely to forget. (And if they do, you can gently remind them.)

As is so often the case in RAM, acting on these opportunities also happens to be the right thing to do. At its best, RAM parallels The Golden Rule in that you treat others the way you want to be treated. That is what creates relationships, bonds, and friendships.

THE PERSON IN THE ROLE

To know stakeholders deeply, in the *conocer* sense of the term, you must think of them as people, with thoughts and feelings similar although not identical to yours. To generate this kind of empathy, put yourself in their place by spoking out and asking yourself questions:

- What are this person's skills, knowledge, and areas of expertise?
- What are his nominal and actual roles in the company?
- What are his major job-related worries?
- What are his major worries off the job?

- What are his short-term and long-term professional and personal ambitions?
- What does he hope to gain by working with me?
- What do his bosses expect of him in his dealings with me?
- How has he triumphed or failed in the past in his work and personal life?
- Who are his allies, friends, competitors, and enemies?
- Does he have the respect he deserves from his co-workers and superiors?

The answer to these and similar questions, together with the information we outlined in Principle #4, will enable you to know the person who is in the role of stakeholder. In your early contacts and when you first spoke out, you won't have the answers to all these questions. However, with open ears, open eyes, and educated guesses, you will eventually obtain most of them.

REAL STAKEHOLDERS

Seeing your stakeholders as people is good for business. It's also great for your social life because business presents a wonderful vehicle for meeting people and getting to know them. However, success in this area, as in other areas of RAM, does require effort.

Bonding with stakeholders isn't rocket science, nor is it mysterious or manipulative. Most businesspeople do it all the time—with their co-workers. Proximity and the common ground of working for the same outfit almost guarantee that will happen. But with RAM strategy, you don't just let relationships happen. You *make* them happen. Creating proximity, out of the office so the person isn't stuck in his role, and finding common ground in your interests and aspirations, will generate personal relationships with most stakeholders.

Keep in mind that although uncountable friendships have started in business, friendship *per se* is not the goal of RAM, or of getting to know your stakeholders as people. When friendships do begin in business, they must be kept in perspective. A manager who can't reprimand an employee or who favors a customer because they are friends is not doing his job. He's also hurting other stakeholders. Rather than friendship, the goal of getting to know your stakeholders as people is to strengthen the business bond. Knowing your stakeholders as people enables you to create more rewarding wins for them, smoother interactions, and longer-term relationships. Those—and the resulting growth and profitability—are the goals of every RAM principle and practice.

POST-GAME WRAP-UP

- Getting to know your stakeholders as people rather than only in their roles as your employees, customers, suppliers, or investors will increase the wins and the fun in doing business with them.
- You'll accelerate the process of bonding with people you meet in business by arranging to see them in nonbusiness settings.
- It's impossible to force a bond between two people, but you can create the conditions in which bonding can occur.
- Use the information you've gathered in making contact and forming a connection to find events, activities, and interests that you and the stakeholder would both enjoy and that would let you get to know one another.
- In maintaining contact, vary the types of touches and also consider frequency, appropriateness, and boundaries.
- Remember that friendship itself is not the goal of building a bond with your stakeholders. Rather, close business relationships enable both stakeholders to achieve more goals, enhance more success factors, and mitigate more risks—and that's the purpose of RAM.

BUILD BONDS OF TRUST WITH ALL STAKEHOLDERS

That is how I perceived the America's Cup being won—by a fantastically tight team. Men who would go to the wall for each other, inspiring, covering, supporting, helping out everywhere, each backing up the others …. Not because they had to, but because they wanted to.

—From Born to Win: A Life-Long Struggle to Capture the America's Cup, *by John Bertrand as told to Patrick Robinson*

In 1983, John Bertrand and his crew captured the America's Cup for Australia, removing it from its hallowed spot in the New York Yacht Club for the first time since America won it from Britain in 1851, and ending Bertrand's 30-year obsession with winning the race. Much of the reason for the underdog crew's victory lay in Bertrand's ability to build an intense level of trust among his crew members. He focused as much on building a confident, cohesive team as he did on the technical preparations for the race. Bertrand was the first skipper ever to employ a sports-psychology program in the America's Cup race, and much of that work was geared toward creating strong bonds among the crew.

Trust is the fundamental bonding agent in every relationship. Businesspeople understand this, which is why brands tout themselves as "the most trusted name in …" and "a name you can trust." In financial services, you'll find trust companies and trust departments, and you'll hear talk of "fiduciary relationships." The term *fiduciary* stems from the Latin *fidere* (to trust), which is also the root of the word *fidelity* (and the dog's name, Fido). Yet despite its importance, businesspeople regularly do things that undermine their stakeholders' trust:

- In 1995, the CEO of Hathaway Shirt Factory in Waterville, Maine, assured his workers that the plant would not close if they "would do quality work and bring down the cost per shirt." Encouraged by the pep talk, employees gave back a recent wage increase and doubled production. Less than 18 months later, the same CEO announced that the factory would be sold, or scrapped if no buyers could be found. The shirts there were not keeping up with the company's other, more profitable lines. Employees elsewhere in the company could be expected to look skeptically upon future assurances from the CEO.

- The March 20, 2000, issue of *Fortune* reported that Naveen Jain, founder and CEO of InfoSpace, a licenser of content to Web sites, sold more than three million shares of his stock in the company for a total of more than $200 million within five months of the IPO. Although he still owned a third of the company after that sale, investment bankers usually insist that founders hold their stock for at least six months, and very often for a year, to show their faith in the company. *Fortune* stated, "Jain's bankers let him jump the gun." Such financial management has not left investors eager for another wave of dot-com IPOs.

- *The Financial Times* reported that DaimlerChrysler Chairman Jurgen Schrempp admitted in the autumn of 2000 that talk of a "merger of equals" with Chrysler "had to be done for psychological reasons. If I had gone and said Chrysler will be a division, everyone on their side would have said, 'There is no way we'll do this deal.'" The so-called cultural problems between the two companies continue to this day.

We could go on, but you probably read the newspaper this morning. Self-dealing, double-talking, and plain old dishonesty are as common in business as in any other profession—perhaps more so, given the temptations and the prevalence of the very non-RAM ethos that someone's win must be someone else's loss. The world being what it is, people often do succeed through untrustworthy means—at least, financially and in the short term. But RAM defines wins beyond the financial and takes a long-term view. In addition, RAM recognizes that people like to associate with and do business with people they trust. The key issue from a RAM perspective, then, is how to build that trust.

TRUST: THE TIE THAT BONDS

Numerous bonds—professional, social, operational, financial, institutional, and cultural—connect businesspeople with one another. The strongest bonds, however, are formed by mutual liking and mutual trust. The liking, as we've pointed out, stems from chemistry—that is, from personal compatibility and shared sensibilities. Those are factors you really can't control. Fortunately, trust is something you can earn, and, in business, being trustworthy is more important than being liked. You can trust someone without liking her, and you can like someone without trusting her. We all know at least one "lovable rogue" with a charming personality and a great line of patter, someone genuinely likable—whom we wouldn't trust with a penny. Meanwhile, some people who exude no personal chemistry for us we would trust with our life savings.

EARNING TRUST

What do you look for in an auto mechanic? We all want a competent mechanic, but most of us are even more concerned about his honesty. The industry has a bad reputation on word-of-mouth from people who have been charged for work that wasn't done or for new parts when they received rebuilt ones, and so on. Mechanics understand this, and the best ones work as hard to build trust—by explaining which repairs are needed now and which can be deferred, and by offering alternatives at various costs—as they do on the cars.

In Principle #2, "Develop a Game Plan," we mentioned that in starting SCG, we knew that we had the ability to deliver and that demand for IT consulting services was strong. We also mentioned our belief that if prospective clients trusted us, they would buy our services often enough for us to build a business. We still see things that way. If you have the expertise and experience *and* the stakeholder trusts you, you'll be able to do business a good percentage of the time.

It takes time to build trust, but the process can be accelerated. If a company is in business for 20 years and sells a good product at a fair price and treats everyone fairly, it will certainly build trust with its stakeholders. But what if you need to grow a business quickly or want to speed up the pace of your career advancement? What if you don't have 20 years to establish trust, which is so crucial to success? Fortunately, you can do things that will establish trust quickly and let you rapidly build on that base—provided that you do them from the initial contact and in every interaction thereafter:

Give trust to get trust: If you approach others in a trusting manner, with a willingness to enter only win-win relationships, you will earn their trust, and you'll deserve it. They will see you taking steps to earn their trust, and they'll respect you for it. RAM builds relationships on the foundation of, "I don't win unless you win, and you don't win unless I win." That's why you can openly begin a discussion with, "Here are ways I think I can win—and ways I think you can win—if we do business together. What do you think?"

The way you approach potential stakeholders largely determines how they respond to you. Your inner feelings about people generally drive your approach. Therefore, you must develop (or strengthen) the belief that people are basically decent and will treat you fairly. If you assume that they will cheat you every chance they get, you will exhibit mistrust in your dealings with people. Trust breeds trust, and suspicion breeds suspicion. This does not mean that you leave yourself open to untrustworthy people. Even with a trusting approach, you must still take steps to protect your interests.

Finally, RAM focuses on getting to know stakeholders as people, and giving and receiving trust is integral to that process. When you get to know someone on a personal level, trust increases exponentially.

Tell the truth: Openness—right from the start—about your business goals and desired wins, your capabilities and resources, and your needs and time frames will foster trust and bring people on board. In our world of hype and overselling, honesty will draw people to you. Conversely, misleading someone about your intentions or capabilities will short-circuit relationships by creating confusion as well as suspicion in stakeholders' minds.

The policy of being truthful must extend to every stakeholder. Stakeholders know one another, run into one another, and can find one another. On the Web and in other media, news travels fast. You can't lie to your employees in one location and have those in another believe you. You can't cash out your stock in your company early and have your customers, employees, and investors keep their faith in its future. You can't say a deal is one thing when you're going into it and then make it another thing when the deal is done, and still expect things to go well.

Keep commitments: When you say you'll call, call. If you make an appointment, keep it. After you agree to a schedule, stick to it. Keeping even small commitments early in a relationship demonstrates that you do what you say you will, and that you expect the same from others. Making only the commitments you can keep will give you a reputation for trustworthiness. Simple stuff, right? Yet so many people treat firm commitments as flexible concepts that all you have to do is faithfully deliver on yours, and you'll achieve a competitive advantage.

Share credit: Recognize others' achievements, even if you've made a major contribution. Generosity with praise and credit can't hurt you—if anything, people might believe you're being falsely modest—and your collaborators will love you for it. Remember the saying, "It's amazing how much you can get done if you're willing to let other people take the credit." Those people will want to work with you because they'll trust you not to grab their share of the praise and rewards.

At SCG, our clients came to trust us because we focused on making *them* look good. The chief information officer and his staff got the credit, and we got the work. We'll take that deal any day.

Criticize constructively: Nobody likes criticism, and people are not wild about critics either. Rein in any urge to find fault with a stakeholder's approach early on, but realize that at times you must correct the actions of an employee, supplier, or other stakeholder. When you do, adopt the role of coach rather than judge. Useful phrases include, "I wonder how it would work if we …" and "Next time, you might try …" and "Could I give you some feedback?" This way, people will trust you not to undercut or humiliate them.

Be a friend: You don't have to co-sign his mortgage, baby-sit his children, or hand him your frequent-flyer miles, but you can offer help when it's appropriate. You can listen when a stakeholder has something to say, even about a personal problem. Offer empathy and, if you're asked, commonsense advice.

Extending a hand to people laid off by our clients and inviting Burger King's IT staff to share our offices during Hurricane Andrew were acts of friendship as well as good RAM practices.

Respect confidences: We mentioned that friendships are built on shared experiences and shared confidences. Revealing something told to you in secret or that you have reason to expect a person would not want revealed betrays a confidence. Few things erode trust faster or more completely. If the subject of a rumor tracks you down as the source, the word embarrassing doesn't begin to describe the situation. Conversely, respecting confidences and keeping secrets brands you as trustworthy and as a friend and confidante.

Provide a proactive win: This is one of the fastest ways to establish trust. When we worked with software vendors to win introductions to their clients, we offered them a proactive, sure-fire win—the tailored demo with the client's data and custom reports—in return for an introduction to the client. Providing that win jump-started the relationship by letting the vendors know they could trust us. A proactive win shows that you trust the stakeholder and truly believe that mutual wins lie ahead.

If you haven't got anything nice to say …: The acid-tongued author Dorothy Parker said, "If you haven't got anything nice to say, sit next to me." It's a great line, but unless you're carving out a career as a literary wit, it's poor advice. In business, follow the traditional wisdom, "If you haven't got anything nice to say, don't say anything." Backbiting undermines listeners' trust in you as they sit there wondering what you say about them when they're not in the room. And you never know who's listening.

An attorney having lunch with a colleague in a restaurant spent a good portion of the meal bad-mouthing a county official of the same political party. He and his colleague were unaware that the official's sister, sitting in the next booth, overheard every word. Several months later when the attorney expressed an interest in running for office, the county official blocked him from the ticket. The attorney found out who had blocked him and approached the official. When they met, the official was, thanks to his sister, able to quote the attorney's remarks back to him.

Incidentally, although the county official might have acted out of revenge, the decision to quash the attorney's candidacy was probably smart politics. Someone unwise enough to publicly bad-mouth a county official (one in the same party, yet, and whose help he might need) might easily be too impolitic to hold office.

Get a reputation: The sum total of what stakeholders know about you, experience with you, and say about you and your organization equals your reputation. Howard Hodgson, a partner in Cabot Industries, states, "Whatever business you are in, you are in a business of relationships. That's why your reputation is your greatest asset."

Doing good work and delivering what you promise will eventually give you a good reputation. However, RAM seeks to *accelerate* word of your reputation and, thus, the trust-building process. In Principle #2, we mentioned that we worked with clients to obtain references and job letters when the engagement went well. These endorsements were so valuable to us that in negotiating the project fee, we sometimes decreased our price in return for them. The client also often permitted us to write up a case study of the project. We used those to help build relationships with the media and draw their attention to our work. When articles appeared about us and our work, we included them in our promotional materials. When a trusted third party, such as a reputable client or a publication as respected as *Information Week* or *Computerworld,* says something good about you, the boost to your reputation can be phenomenal. When prospective clients saw those job letters hanging on the wall in our reception area, and when they received excellent references from our past and present clients, they knew those people trusted us. That encouraged them to trust us, too.

CAN YOU BE TOO TRUSTING?

As thousands of swindled individuals learn every year, the answer to this question is "Yes." When you evaluate a potential stakeholder, judge his trustworthiness by the statements and actions unearthed by your research. Get a feel for the character of an organization's management. Note any lawsuits and judgments against the company. Always check references. Ask yourself: Who are the company's stakeholders? How does the company treat customers, suppliers, creditors, and the community? What do former stakeholders say about the company? Does the company cut corners? Is money the only goal? Does the company make long-term commitments, or does it churn customers, encourage turnover, and switch suppliers as though people were interchangeable?

Although RAM focuses on building trust, the approach is always businesslike. That means never abandoning practices such as written contracts, solid documentation, and sound legal advice. At times, someone might try to put things on a personal level by saying something like, "You know, our relationship is so strong that we don't need a contract. We can do this deal on a handshake." Never go along with that idea. Guard yourself against anyone who uses the personal side of a relationship to conduct business in an unbusinesslike way. People who are serious about keeping their commitments—in other words, trustworthy people—have no qualms about putting their commitments in writing. Even if the person means well by suggesting a deal on a handshake or a similar notion, it's a bad idea.

Never take a company's size or success as evidence of its trustworthiness. In the late 1980s, a computer networking firm (which we'll call by the fictitious name Networx) struck an agreement with a software giant (which we'll call Softcode, another fictitious name) that allowed Softcode to sell some of its network products in certain markets. Networx wanted to expand its market, and Softcode wanted networking solutions among its offerings. It looked like a win-win situation. As part of the deal, Softcode agreed not to sell network products to Networx's customers.

Before long, Networx learned that Softcode was violating the agreement. Softcode was indeed selling network products to those off-limits customers. Networx called Softcode on the violation and was told that the contract was so vague that the networking firm had no case. The deal, which would have significantly helped Networx, ultimately hurt the company. The CEO who made the agreement was ousted.

Later, in an off-the-record conversation, a Softcode executive told the Networx CEO, "You made a mistake."

"What was that?" the CEO asked.

"You trusted us," said the software executive.

Evidently, Softcode believed that the gains of violating the agreement were worth the price paid in lost trust. However, the company seriously damaged its reputation as a trustworthy partner and left other companies extremely wary of entering alliances with it.

A person's or a company's ethics, values, and view of business dictate the bounds of fair play. Many businesspeople believe in *caveat emptor*—let the buyer beware—and "Do unto others before they do unto you." They see business as a contact sport not in the sense that we mean it—as an endeavor in which success depends on close contacts—but rather as *mano-a-mano* competition. In the world of athletics, boxing is the ultimate contact sport. Two men (or women, a recent trend) in a prizefight know they must keep their guard up, hit hard, and knock out their opponent. You accept those rules when you step into the ring. Some people, such as the software executive who said, "You made a mistake. You trusted us," believe in similar rules for business. Keep your guard up, hit hard, and knock 'em out. They often assume that you hold the same view. They don't trust you, so they don't expect to be trusted. They care only about their own wins and believe that you care only about yours. They don't want a long-term relationship, and they figure you're in for the short term, too. From a RAM perspective, there is no reason to enter relationships with people who think this way.

FROM THE RAM PLAYBOOK

Check references, but not in a perfunctory manner. Virtually all parties supply only names of people who will give positive references. And people called for references are understandably wary about providing negative information. However, try to break through by saying, "This is a very important _____ (hire, transaction, contract, or whatever) for us. That's why I'm taking my time and yours to check on this person's past performance. I'd like to spend a few minutes on the phone with you learning about how this person came to you, why you chose to do business with him, how he performed, the amount of value you derived, and the nature of the relationship you had with him."

Then ask probing, open-ended questions on each of these topics. Wait for the whole answer, and then wait to see if the person adds more information. If you impress upon the reference the importance of accurate information, you'll stand a better chance of getting it. To give the person a win, offer to provide the same level of candor when she calls you.

Another technique that sometimes produces openness is to frame the talk in third-party terms. Try something like, "We all know that no one gets along perfectly with everyone. Among people who didn't always get along with Jim, what were their reasons?" That way, the person giving the reference can lay off negative news on the nameless third parties.

TRUST THE PROCESS

Practitioners of creative arts, such as acting, filmmaking, and fiction writing, will talk about trusting the creative process. Doctors will tell their patients who are on the mend to trust the healing process. We say trust the Relationship Asset Management process. When it's properly practiced, RAM is a process businesspeople can trust. Why? Because an energetic, skillful, persistent search for mutual wins can have only one of two outcomes: the discovery of mutual wins or the failure to find them. In the former case, you can do business. In the latter, you can't.

The moral underpinnings of Relationship Asset Management make the process one you can trust. RAM rests on the principle that people enter business transactions for mutual gain, believing that the relationship will be a fair exchange of value for value rather than attempting to exploit one another to receive value for nothing. Implicit in RAM is the notion that exploitative relationships have bad outcomes, no matter who does the exploiting. ("In a rat race, even the winner is a rat.") If you are the exploited party, it's a lose-win relationship, and it doesn't even make short-term sense. If you are doing the exploiting, the relationship will soon turn sour, and so will a part of your reputation.

FROM THE RAM PLAYBOOK

We've found that RAM's long-term, win-win focus keeps us out of trouble. For instance, at Entente Investment, our RAM strategy dictated a longer-term viewpoint than many other venture investors adopted at the time. We targeted as potential investments only start-ups or early stage firms that were doing IT consulting for Fortune 1000 companies; handling traditional back-end applications, such as inventory management and accounting, as well as (or instead of) Web-based applications; and presenting sensible business plans.

This was at the height of the Internet IPO craze, well before the tech-stock meltdown in 2000. In those days, we met a number of entrepreneurs who said things like, "We want to build the company to 5 offices and 300 employees as fast as we can, regardless of losses, and then go public." We avoided those deals like the plague, not because we had a crystal ball but because we had a long-term view and a process we trusted. With that view and process, we pursued 6 attractive investments in our first 18 months of operating Entente, and we landed all 6.

Given that trust is essential to relationships, how can it ever make sense to trade away a stakeholder's trust for a short-term financial gain? If someone lies about an important product feature to make a sale or cuts corners to boost his profit on a job, he's undercutting the stakeholder's trust and, thus, the longer-term relationship and his own reputation—both of which ultimately have more value.

Being trustworthy is good business. It encourages trustworthiness in stakeholders and sets high standards of behavior for the relationship. People who trust one another can eliminate the suspicion, secretiveness, blame games, and coverup tactics that hinder progress. They can more quickly define and develop mutual wins because they trust that neither one wants the other to lose. All these benefits result from implementing RAM throughout your Relationship Web, sometimes only on faith.

THE VALUE OF TRUST AMONG STAKEHOLDERS

The recent case of Ford and Firestone vividly demonstrates the value of trust among suppliers, employees, customers, shareholders, government agencies, the media, and the community—by illustrating its rapid erosion. On August 2, 2000, the National Highway Transportation Administration announced an investigation of deaths related to Firestone tires and Ford Explorers. About a week later, Bridgestone/Firestone announced a recall of 6.5 million tires. Some two thirds of the tires were on Ford SUVs and trucks.

Ford and Firestone had been doing business since their earliest days. The relationship went back 100 years to their founders, Henry Ford and Harvey Firestone, who had been friends and close business associates. Regarding the recall, Ford and Firestone initially supported one another. The August 10 issue of *The New York Times* noted, "Ford said it still stood by its supplier."

Things deteriorated rapidly from there. On August 13, Ford released documents showing that Firestone received complaints about treads separating from tires in 1997. Ford also cited the tire company's

Decatur, Illinois, plant as the main source of the problem tires. On August 14, the *Times* reported, "Until now Ford and Firestone sought to present a united front. But several disclosures indicate that their relationship is being strained by the tire recall."

Congressional committee hearings worsened the strain. The *Times* quoted Sen. Ernest Hollings saying that the hearing was "like tying two cats by the tail and throwing them over the clothesline and letting them claw each other." Ford CEO Jacques Nasser stated that Firestone knew of problems with the tires, "yet Firestone said nothing to anyone, including Ford Motor Company." Firestone executive John Lampe countered with accusations that the design of the Explorer was the major cause of the accidents.

Firestone workers at the Decatur plant weighed in with mixed messages. Some pointed to the many "Quality One" awards from Ford over the years. However, others cited heavy production demands and lax quality control as basic causes of the tire trouble. Some traced the problems back to poor supervision of the tire-making process and poor training of new workers after a bitter 10-month strike that ended in May 1995.

The debacle had far-reaching effects. Bridgestone took a record $350 million charge against earnings to cover the costs of the recall. The company's stock price had plummeted almost 30 percent by then. In October, 450 workers at the Decatur factory were indefinitely laid off, and that factory and two others were temporarily closed. The overall media blitz prompted thousands of new complaints to government agencies about the tires and the vehicles.

Whatever the lapses on the part of each company were, their quickness to turn on one another undermined trust between them and their stakeholders—consumers, employees, investors, and government agencies. Although RAM might not have prevented the tragic deaths in this case, RAM would have called for accepting responsibility and dealing with the matter quickly and to everyone's satisfaction. Also, there could have been ways to maintain the trust the two companies had enjoyed for a century. First, true stakeholders share information as fully as they can. Second, they work to solve problems together. Third, they don't blame one another, certainly not in public or before the media. Finally, they listen to stakeholders who have valuable information for them.

BUILDING A TRUSTING TEAM

How do you construct a team like the one John Bertrand put together to win the America's Cup? We believe that RAM builds trust because each deal must be win-win and every stakeholder counts. RAM has worked for us. Similar approaches to stakeholders at other companies have created similar results.

For instance, Sean McLaughlin, founder and CEO of Eze Castle, a Boston-based software supplier for top Wall Street firms, discusses what he calls the Three R's of integrity: reputation, results, and reliability. "These are the three things we expect," he says, "and the three things our clients need to see from us. If anyone lets us down in one of these areas, it affects all of us." McLaughlin believes that building trust is, from a business perspective, practical and efficient: "If you can trust people and they trust you, life becomes a hell of a lot simpler. A trusting environment lowers the conflicts and political issues in a company. And trust is something everybody wants to feel."

McLaughlin explains the company's work ethic and concept of loyalty to all prospective employees. It's not a 9-to-5 shop, but employees receive excellent compensation and growth opportunities. In return, they are asked to contribute extraordinary effort from time to time. Those times test their loyalty to the company, and they are expected to step up just as the company does for them. The approach must be working. *Mass High Tech (The Journal of New England Technology)* cites Eze Castle as one of the 10 fastest-growing companies in Massachusetts.

However a company goes about it, building relationships on trust will take a team farther, with a greater sense of self-respect and integrity, than any other way of doing business.

- Trust is essential to good business relationships, yet people regularly make decisions and take actions that undermine their stakeholders' trust.

- Mutual liking and mutual trust form the strongest bonds between people. Mutual liking either occurs or doesn't occur, as a matter of chemistry. But trust can be earned.

- You can take many actions to establish and build trust, including making only commitments you can keep, sharing credit, respecting confidences, and supplying a win proactively. Working with customers and the media to build your reputation can accelerate the trust-building process.

- Trust everyone, but cut the cards. Always know who you are doing business with, check their references thoroughly, and understand how they view the boundaries and unwritten rules of the game.

- The RAM process reinforces trust because practitioners enter only win-win relationships and avoid exploiting others as diligently as they avoid being exploited. These moral underpinnings of RAM render the process itself trustworthy.

- The reputation of a person or company is the sum total of what stakeholders know, feel, experience, and say about that person or company. Therefore, any negative knowledge, feeling, experience, or statement in any quarter detracts from that person's or company's reputation.

BANISH RELATIONSHIP KILLERS

John Rocker's remarks about Mets fans and New York residents in general have put his future as the Atlanta Braves' [star relief pitcher] in peril. The remarks, which were ethnically and racially offensive in tone, have ignited a firestorm of protest and condemnation of Rocker from his teammates and residents of Atlanta. … Jim Schultz, the Braves public relations director, said the Braves' offices were swamped with calls on Wednesday …. "Half a dozen or so threatened to cancel their season tickets. A lot of people said they'd never watch a Braves game on TV."

—From *"Remarks Could Hurt Rocker Most of All,"* The New York Times, *December 24, 1999*

In sports or in business, a single mistake can cost the entire team the game—or, as in the case of John Rocker's comments in *Sports Illustrated,* valuable stakeholders. Even when the damage can be contained, such a mistake often alters a relationship forever and diminishes the value of the underlying asset for both parties. Mistakes in early stage relationships are usually more costly than those in established ones. New relationships provide less context and lower reserves of trust, goodwill, and mutual knowledge to draw upon in repairing the damage. Without that context, a breach of taste, etiquette, boundaries, or ethics can be extremely hard to overcome. But even long-term relationships cannot withstand the more serious mistakes, such as betrayal.

For all these reasons, we call the mistakes that we examine in this chapter relationship killers. If that strikes you as dramatic, that's okay. Business and personal relationships at all stages of development die every day. That's sad, but it's sadder still that one party often doesn't even know why the relationship died or failed to thrive. Many of us are shadowed by a relationship killer (or two—they often travel in pairs) for most of our lives, neither knowing it nor calculating the cost to ourselves and others. So, a bit of drama might underscore the importance of avoiding these mistakes in the first place.

To ease into this sensitive area, we'll start with mistakes that emerge from the conduct of the relationship itself, the mechanics of the business relationship. We call these Type I relationship killers. Then we'll cover killers that lurk in our personalities, in our beliefs about others and our behavior toward them. As you might imagine, apprehending the first kind of killer is easier than arresting the second. Yet in both cases, RAM strategy will work far more quickly and effectively if you first recognize, and second avoid, these mistakes.

TYPE I RELATIONSHIP KILLERS

People enter business (and personal) relationships with certain needs, desires, and expectations. Generally, the closer the match between each party's needs, desires, and expectations—and in their ability to fulfill those of one another—the more smoothly the relationship will run and the more value it will accrue over time.

Type I relationship killers arise primarily out of misunderstandings on one or both sides regarding needs, desires, or expectations, and out of lapses in executing basic RAM practices. These killers include the following:

- Poor preparation
- Lack of focus
- False expectations
- Win-lose relationships
- Lack of ownership
- Poor maintenance

POOR PREP IS A MISSTEP

We covered pregame preparation in detail in Principle #4, "Transform Contacts into Connections." Here we emphasize the importance of doing your homework. Gathering information on a potential stakeholder and identifying potential wins *before* a meeting forestalls the "clueless" approach to relationship development. Although being nicely dressed and personable certainly helps, you can go only so far with, "I'm a nice guy. You're a nice guy."

We mentioned our strategy for leveraging the sales forces of software vendors who were calling on the companies that we wanted to do business with. First, we had to identify those vendors. As noted, we looked to the areas that were hot at the time—financial systems, sales force automation, data warehousing, and enterprise resource planning—and then identified the top vendors in each of those areas. We also targeted the fastest-growing vendors, reasoning that they would be open to ideas for increasing their sales and would have an approach to business that was compatible with ours. The win that we wanted, which we had identified from our analysis of our goals, success factors, and risks, was access to potential buyers of our services.

When we approached a vendor, we were prepared for a serious discussion. Because we had no complementary software or hardware to sell, the major win that we felt we could give was leads to our clients and prospects. That was the win that we decided to provide up front, and we hoped for a corresponding win in return: leads to the vendor's customers and prospects. When we met with a vendor, the information and the approach that we had developed beforehand positioned us as potential partners with something to offer.

In business, as in all things, the Five P's apply: Proper Planning Prevents Poor Performance.

FUZZY FOCUS ALWAYS FAILS

As we've seen, it takes a series of moves for two parties to go from contact to connection and a solid relationship. When initial efforts to move things forward seem stalled, often neither party has closed the sale (literally or figuratively). A business relationship requires a focus, usually centered on making or saving money. While nonmonetary wins have value in themselves, even they often translate to money earned or saved down the road.

Businesspeople respond to people who are focused. If one party focuses on moving forward, the other party will usually do the same—or decline to do so. Useful phrases include, "So, where are we going with this?" and "When will you be ready to take the next step?" and "What will it take for you to feel comfortable moving ahead?" If these questions fail to draw a positive response, either your focus is fuzzy or you haven't made the wins for the other party clear enough or compelling enough.

Bring those wins into sharper focus. Often this means discovering the other party's biggest problem or "hot button"—the thing *he's* most focused on. For example, the very first software vendor that we approached liked us and liked the idea of swapping leads with us. As the meeting progressed, we moved toward an informal agreement to share leads. Many agreements of this type, though well-intentioned, fail to bear fruit because they're too vague. We all wanted something more focused, so the president introduced us to his sales manager and we continued talking. When the sales manager described the way his salespeople did their demos with canned data on Acme Inc. and widgets, a light went on in Tom Richardson's head. "What if your salespeople could demonstrate the software with data and reports customized for the company they were trying to sell to?" he asked.

It hit the sales manager immediately, and we realized that there was a concrete win that we at SCG could start giving them next week. With that focus, we were able to move forward and get the vendor's agreement to have us customize the demos. In return, the sales manager agreed to introduce us to the prospect so that we could pitch our consulting services.

The goal of a business relationship is not simple fellowship. It is mutual wins with a financial payoff. When that focus is missing or lost, the relationship has nowhere to go and thus has no momentum. When compelling wins have been identified, momentum picks up. You maintain that momentum by shifting the focus to action steps needed to achieve them. Then you're both working together toward the same objective.

YOU CAN'T STAY TRUE TO FALSE EXPECTATIONS

Expecting something that will never materialize guarantees disappointment. That's why RAM emphasizes open discussion of each party's wins *and* each party's obligation to deliver wins. Openness about wins and contributions defuses false expectations, or at least uncovers them. Don't view false expectations as a sign of bad faith. They usually arise out of one party's normal way of doing business or their preconceived assumptions about the deal.

For instance, we've found that many people in business expect some form of exclusivity as a win. That expectation can be hard to meet. When we partnered with software vendors, we found that most of them wanted an exclusive arrangement. However, our business model, which depended on multiple vendor relationships, made this impossible. So we compromised. When a vendor wanted exclusivity, we instead agreed that when the vendor introduced us to a prospect, we would carry that vendor's flag to the end. We agreed that if another vendor's product was selected, we would bow out with the losing vendor. In these instances, if the client asked us to implement the selected software solution, we would ask the vendor who brought us in if they would mind if we did the work. If they minded, we passed up the job. If they didn't mind, we took it on. This commitment was our alternative to exclusivity, and we lived up to it. It was key to building a reputation as a reliable partner.

Unrealistic expectations also commonly arise around pricing. Many prospective clients want assurances of "the lowest price." You can't promise everyone the lowest price without disappointing someone. Our solution at SCG was to outline explicit price breaks based on volume. This enabled us to treat all clients equitably while casting the matter of pricing as a potential win for both parties—if we got more work, the client got a better rate.

Unfortunately, some people actually prefer muddled expectations. They see greater upside potential if things aren't "nailed down." Or, they intend to increase their demands later in the process. Or, they believe that they can slide by with lower-quality, mediocre service, or missed deadlines if those parameters are left unclear. This reasoning is faulty for three reasons: First, the upside potential rarely materializes, and, if it might, the shares should be explicitly agreed upon beforehand. Second, making demands beyond original expectations erodes trust, appears greedy, and leaves one party feeling as if they have been treated unfairly. Third, mediocre performance will kill any relationship. Plus, why try to live down to rather than up to expectations?

WIN-LOSE KILLS THE GOOSE

No long-term relationship can develop if one party has been set up to lose. This occurs constantly between buyers and suppliers—one pushes the other on price, depending on which one has the upper hand at the time. Such power plays are short-sighted because market conditions inevitably change, shifting power to the party that lost last time. Then that party wants its turn to cut the other guy's throat. It's a poor foundation for a relationship.

A well-known nationwide retailing chain was infamous for backing its suppliers to the wall on price. By forcing them to sell at painfully low margins, the retailer created an adversarial relationship based solely on the economics of the situation. In effect, the retailer said, "We own the field, the ball, and the bat. You want to play here? Play by our rules."

One Christmas season, the chain's store managers found themselves very short of a very popular series of stuffed character dolls. Kids were driving their parents through the roof over these dolls, and parents did the same to the price of the item. Faced with empty shelves and irate customers, the retailer's buyers hit the phones and begged their suppliers for a shipment of the dolls. These calls came up empty. Those profit-starved suppliers just weren't able to get their hands on enough of those toys to go around that Christmas.

Regardless of the stakeholders involved, adversarial business practices work against relationships. People who use them don't view relationships as long-term assets.

NO OWNERSHIP EQUALS NO STAKEHOLDER

Relationships without owners die. It's that simple. Moreover, relationship owners must see themselves as owners and must act the part. Aside from applying RAM principles to their dealings with stakeholders, this involves making a smooth hand-off to the new owner when moving on to a new position or employer. Surprisingly, many companies allow people to move to a new internal position without preparing successors to handle their relationships well. Worse, people leaving the company might take relationships with them, most often those with customers or other employees.

Our solution at SCG and in more recent ventures has been twofold. First, we establish one owner with primary responsibility for the relationship asset, as well as co-ownership by the CRO. We also foster a sense of ownership among other people on the stakeholder's team. Second, we establish transfer procedures, similar to those applied to an employee's keys, data files, and deal-making authority. We also use noncompete agreements, which offer additional, though not total, protection against customers leaving along with employees.

A relationship management team with breadth and depth represents the best insurance against orphaned stakeholders, or lack of ownership.

POOR MAINTENANCE CAUSES BREAKDOWNS

All relationships demand maintenance, typically in the form of personal contact. If people work for you, do business with you, or invest in you without regular contact, don't assume that everything's fine. Without that contact, most stakeholders sooner or later get that taken-for-granted feeling. Neglect stands among the most common relationship killers. (Think about the relationships you've lost.)

Proper maintenance happens only when systems *and* accountability support the effort. No system will operate itself, but without a system, relationship owners will inevitably let some details of maintenance slip past them. To hold owners truly accountable, you must have systems—of information management, touch schedules, and feedback—that both support them and track their efforts.

Finally, proper maintenance means maintaining the wins as well as the communications. Assessing relationships for the balance of the wins at least twice a year keeps each party aware of the balance. When a customer defects or a licensee doesn't renew a contract or an investor pulls out, the balance of the wins has deteriorated in that party's view—probably without you even noticing it. We view any customer defection, employee resignation, concerned investor, or negative press as a requisition for maintenance. As with auto and health maintenance, you want to catch small problems before they become big problems.

FROM THE RAM PLAYBOOK

Don't be a victim. If you see a relationship killer shadowing a potential stakeholder, carefully weigh the positives and negatives and the potential value and costs. Sometimes, particularly in inherently temporary relationships, you can survive even when the relationship doesn't. But that's not our approach or recommendation. Even in temporary relationships, people often say, "It wasn't worth the headaches."

It's best to avoid relationships that are doomed to failure, not because you or your organization will necessarily suffer irreparable harm (although it's possible). The real reason is the forgone opportunity to develop a relationship with a stakeholder who will bring more to the table, treat you well, and, in all likelihood, develop into a better business partner than the one you thought you had to put up with for some reason. In a properly run business, no one is irreplaceable.

Also, enduring difficult relationships exacts a cost on an organization. For instance, employees who must deal with irrational customers or uncooperative suppliers feel (correctly) that they're being treated poorly and that management isn't backing them up. This creates an automatic lose-win situation for the employees who must deal with the difficult parties, and it erodes the value of the relationship with employees.

On the subject of balancing the wins, we know a vendor who occasionally gives a client a discount that was not negotiated up front. He bills by the project rather than for time, and if a job takes substantially less time than he anticipated, he bills the client below the agreed-upon amount. That doesn't happen often—only when he feels the wins tipping too far toward him. This vendor charges top dollar and knows that competitors regularly pitch to his clients. It would be easy to underprice him, so providing these wins proactively helps forestall customer defections.

Type I relationship killers arise out of business situations, and from failure to apply RAM principles fully and faithfully. Any of these killers can end a relationship if they show up often enough or hit with enough force. Even so, they are, by and large, easier to avoid or address than Type II killers.

TYPE II RELATIONSHIP KILLERS

Type II relationship killers arise from our beliefs about or behaviors toward other people. They reside in the personality, and that makes them harder to identify and often more deadly. They tend to be more hurtful than purely "business-based" Type I relationship killers in that people take them more personally. Moreover, most people avoid rather than point out these killers because these faults are more personal and thus more difficult to discuss. Therefore, they must be caught and eliminated by each of us. Type II relationship killers include these:

- Poor hygiene and social shortcomings
- Personality problems
- Breached boundaries
- Prejudicial attitudes
- Betrayal

POOR HYGIENE AND SOCIAL SHORTCOMINGS

Even today, in the supposedly image-obsessed United States, we have all witnessed alarming cases of poor grooming and poor hygiene. These can take a staggering array of forms, which we need not review here. (Suffice it to say that we're aware of subordinates staying late at the office to place bottles of Listerine or Head and Shoulders on their managers' desks—not in any of our enterprises, of course.)

Not everyone has great looks, perfect manners, fascinating anecdotes, and oodles of charm. Most businesspeople accept that. However, actual social shortcomings can damage relationships or prevent their formation. Top killers include an overbearing physical or psychological presence, compulsive touching, vulgarity, swearing, and an overabundance of "attitude." Drinking and smoking to excess and illegal drug use are killers in every way.

In all relationships, the fundamental rule of good manners is consideration for others. You don't start eating until everyone is served so that you're truly dining together rather than racing for a second helping. You cough into your left hand because you shake hands with your right. You might not know the difference between a salad fork and an oyster fork, and you might not realize that you're supposed to taste your food before you salt it, but if you have genuine consideration for others, you'll do well.

Here's what we mean: President Dwight D. Eisenhower once hosted a formal state dinner, complete with fine China, crystal stemware, and finger bowls. The guest of honor was a dignitary from Japan, where finger bowls were not customarily used. Early on, the guest of honor picked up his finger bowl and drank out of it. Some guests froze. Others tried to hide their amusement. Meanwhile, Eisenhower raised his finger bowl to his lips, took a sip of water, and set all of his guests at ease.

PERSONALITY PROBLEMS

Some relationships endure despite one party making the other miserable. The offended party sticks around for the wins, but the minute they are gone, so is the relationship. Many of us—particularly as the population ages and more people get too old for this stuff—factor in the costs of dealing with "head cases" and other difficult types when we're considering a business relationship. Life's too short and business is challenging enough without those complications.

We all have ways of looking at this issue. New York literary agent Richard Curtis calls it the PITA Factor, which he uses to gauge a prospective Pain In The Ass. Other people grade employees, bosses, contractors, or business partners on "works and plays well with others." Talented people quickly move on when exposed to abusive, arrogant, inflexible, self-centered, petty, or otherwise unreasonable people. Everyone has quirks, and nobody's perfect. However, if you've been "spoken to" about "being difficult" it would be a good idea—at a moment when you're open to hearing what could be the awful truth—to ask a trusted colleague for some candid feedback regarding your style of interacting with others.

More than a few difficult people have benefited from counseling, coaching, behavior modification, or insight coupled with plain old will power. Yet the existence of books such as *How to Work for a Jerk* and *Work Would Be Great If It Weren't for the People* indicate that not everyone in business has taken full advantage of these remedies.

FROM THE RAM PLAYBOOK

Executive coaches spend a fair amount of their billable time helping people, usually senior managers, eliminate Type II relationship killers. This involves helping the executive to recognize and overcome—or, at least, compensate for—personal or managerial shortcomings. Companies refer executives to coaches (sometimes as a condition of promotion or continued employment) because these problems can kill relationships with stakeholders, and those relationships are key to the company's success and the manager's success.

Among the most common problems are: abrupt, arrogant, and bullying behavior; "inappropriate" humor and comments; sexual innuendos and harassment; anger management; poor listening skills; lack of empathy; micromanagement and inability to delegate; inability to focus on, plan, and complete large tasks; adult attention deficit disorder; eating disorders, and alcohol and other substance abuse.

Effective approaches include testing to determine the nature and source of the problem; feedback and biofeedback; hypnosis; group discussion and therapy; sensitivity and diversity training; managerial skills training; and for addiction, rehabilitation, behavior modification, and 12-step programs.

In small firms and family-owned companies, senior managers must be certain to ask for and give one another honest feedback about their problems. Ironically enough, those companies provide more cover for managers with problems than large ones because the problematic person might be the CEO, the founder, or a major investor.

BREACHING BOUNDARIES

As previously noted, each of us maintains physical, social, and psychological boundaries that help us maintain our well-being. Violating boundaries, knowingly or otherwise, can end a relationship before it begins. Ironically, the violation often occurs out of friendliness or enthusiasm. For instance, "space invaders" typically mean well. They want to get to know you, so they share (or request) information that you'd rather not discuss, make themselves at home in your office, and read your e-mails over your shoulder. Some of these folks are nosy. Some, such as those who always seem to want a ride to the airport, are self-serving. However, most of the time they are merely thoughtless.

Violators of social boundaries lack the patience and maturity to let a relationship take its natural course. They pitch deals to people at social functions and then wonder why they're not invited back. They become abusive of receptionists and other gatekeepers when a relationship does not take flight immediately, and thus shut themselves out forever. Boundary violators cause damage as well as irritation. For example, representing yourself as "a friend of George Soros" because you were introduced to him at a function by a mutual friend can damage your friend's relationship with Mr. Soros and your relationship with your friend.

The "network overstep" creates similar problems. Using the name of a friend, acquaintance, or contact without his permission can open doors—to trouble. If you find yourself unwilling to ask someone for an introduction or for permission to use their name to contact someone else, ask yourself why. Do you really have a potential win to offer the person you're trying to reach? Do you know your acquaintance well enough, or, more to the point, does he know you well enough for you to ask this favor? Do you fear that he will refuse, and, if so, why? Just using "a name" to gain access to someone can work, but it will generally work against you.

Social boundaries used to be clearer. For example, the old rule of dinner conversation said never to discuss politics, religion, or other men's wives. Placing highly charged topics off-limits helped make for a pleasant evening. Breaching these or other boundaries, particularly if you're no longer at an age where people might chalk it up to the brashness of youth, can place you permanently out of bounds. But although you must avoid physically or virtually invading someone's space, you must make a connection. Determining the amount of contact needed to build a connection without invading someone's space is an art best learned through experience.

PREJUDICIAL ATTITUDES

Business brings you in contact with a wide range of people. To connect with a wide range of people, you must be able to relate to them. This could mean recognizing your preconceived notions about certain groups of people so that you can see those people clearly. Then you can focus on mutual wins rather than their nationality, gender, or accent.

Executive development consultant Paul Miller points out, "By understanding your prejudices about others, you are better able to tune in to those people as people because you'll be able to tune out the static caused by those attitudes." Regardless of your own characteristics, if you judge others based on their color, sex, appearance, accent, socioeconomic class, marital status, political affiliation, place in the organization, or technical specialty, you'll find it harder to connect with them. Those superficial differences are exactly that—differences—and connections arise from a focus on commonalities rather than differences.

Openness—toward people, possibilities, and opportunities—is involved in every aspect of RAM. Therefore, you must be aware of your preconceptions and tune them out—or, failing that, allow for them and dismiss their possible effect on your ability to see others clearly. Ideally, we would all rid ourselves of these attitudes.

BETRAYAL

This is the deadliest relationship killer because trust is the basis of every relationship. Betray a trust, and you undermine the relationship's foundation. Betrayal can range from failing to meet expectations to not sharing vital information, to reneging on promises, to rumor-mongering, double-crossing, or back-stabbing.

Integrity, which precludes betrayal, comes in many forms. It's there when a company that knows that it will be late with a delivery faces that fact and warns the customer. It's there in a set of realistic financial projections for banks and investors. It's there in quality materials and solid workmanship when cheaper would be "good enough." It's there when people say what they will do and then do it.

Business has always had—and always will have—its share of greed, fraud, lying, exploitation, and corner-cutting. Some men and women engaged in these practices have built considerable fortunes, but they haven't built valuable relationships, which would allow them to be successful intimately.

THE CASE FOR CIVILITY

Rome wasn't built in a day, but it took only a day to burn it down. Similarly, relationship assets developed over years can be lost in an instant. Early stage relationships are even more fragile. Therefore, civility in manners, respect for others, and openness about expectations represent the fundamentals of RAM at the person-to-person level.

Many people, including ourselves, are concerned about the lack of civility in our society. Politics has become a blood sport. Business places profits above all other goals. Family life is under siege. We believe that Relationship Asset Management, though it is essentially a business strategy, embodies a formula for greater civility. The bedrock principle is the

Golden Rule—treat others as you want to be treated. Be friendly and ready to see everyone as a potential partner in a worthwhile endeavor. Be open about your desires and honest about what you can contribute. And do everything possible to deliver on every commitment that you make.

POST-GAME WRAP-UP

- Type I relationship killers tend to arise from business matters rather than personal ones. Most of these barriers to good relationships can be addressed by putting RAM practices—setting expectations precisely, conducting proper maintenance, and so on—into action.
- Type II relationship killers arise more from personal beliefs and behaviors. These killers are usually harder to deal with because they arise from our personalities.
- Often people are shadowed by a relationship killer all their lives without knowing it. Self-examination, as well as listening to feedback from others, can help you identify any that might be tailing you.
- Executive coaches and other professionals, as well as particularly good managers and mentors, can usually help someone address their own Type II relationship killers.
- The deadliest relationship killer is betrayal because it undermines trust, which is the foundation of every relationship, business or personal.

PRINCIPLE #9:

WHEN SOMETHING BREAKS, FIX IT FAST

[Seven Miami Dolphins were holding out for higher salaries. Things reached a head when two of them decided not to report to training camp.] Three days later the players met with [general manager and superb negotiator] Joe Robbie. … "There wasn't an angry word exchanged," revealed Robbie. "We weren't slapping each other on the back and saying rah, rah, rah, but there wasn't any anger involved either. We talked serious business. I stressed to them that we are on the same side; our futures were tied together, the future of the Miami Dolphins. I think they agree with me on that."

—*From* Miracle in Miami: The Miami Dolphins Story, *by Lou Sahadi*

In professional sports, the games played off the field, involving salaries, trades, contracts, working conditions, and potential strikes, can be as fascinating—and as bruising—as the games on the field. Whenever relationships between club owners and players break down, the owners, players, fans, and the whole game suffer. We all saw this most recently in the NBA players' walkout for much of the 1998–99 season and, before that, in the labor dispute that canceled the 1994 World Series.

RAM aims to avoid broken relationships by means of regular maintenance. When maintenance fails and a problem does occur, early detection will often keep a small problem from growing into a large one. In most situations, the earlier people start working on a problem, the sooner it is solved and the less damage it causes. However, even RAM cannot prevent the occasional total breakdown of a relationship, which is why we include ways of repairing them as a principle of the system.

Also, we've found that whenever we speak to business audiences, the subject of fixing broken relationships comes up. How do you know when there's trouble in a relationship before someone explodes or quietly heads for the door? How can you learn what's wrong when a stakeholder starts drifting away? How do you actually get a derailed relationship back on track?

In this principle, we examine ways of diagnosing what's wrong in a business relationship and how to go about fixing what's wrong. Much of the material assumes that you (or your company), rather than the stakeholder, has caused the break in the relationship. A later section in this chapter assumes that the stakeholder has caused the break.

FINDING WHAT'S BROKEN

We believe that it's much easier to fix broken business relationships than people realize. However, you do have to identify what's wrong before you can fix it. Problems can range from mere thoughtlessness or minor offenses up to serious disagreements about the balance of the wins. Moreover, some problems seem to take on a life of their own and quickly become difficult to analyze unless you know how to go about it. Here we offer some guidelines on exactly that. Yet even with these tools, it will take detective work—and good communication within the company and often with the stakeholder—to find the source of trouble.

WHAT'S THE PROBLEM?

In the late 1990s, a defense contractor had a department of dissatisfied chip designers. The chips it designed went into missile guidance systems and were produced to strict government specifications. The work was extremely important, but, at the time, these were not the most glamorous high-tech jobs or the most highly paid. As a bureaucracy, the defense contractor had a fairly rigid compensation system that could not match the astronomical salaries, bonuses, and stock-option plans prevalent in the high-tech job market at the time.

One day, about 20 designers got together and presented the CEO with an ultimatum: Give us a 30 percent pay increase, or we leave for higher-paying positions outside the defense industry.

Management heard this wake-up call and brought in an organizational consultant to help address the situation. The consultant listened to the designers' complaints about the pay structure and their tales of the money they could be making elsewhere. Then, knowing that nonfinancial wins often mean more to highly skilled professionals than money, he asked them to imagine certain ideal conditions unrelated to salary. He suggested several, such as the company demonstrating a true corporate commitment to developing leading-edge technologies, giving the designers time and support for research activities, letting them provide input regarding the direction of the organization, and so on. They considered these conditions and added a couple of their own.

Then the consultant said, "It's quite possible that the company could not do this, but if all these conditions could be met right here, how much money would it take to lure you away from your current positions?" Most of the designers said it would take at least double their salaries to get them even to consider leaving such a company. Several said that no amount of money would lure them away.

This meeting pointed the way toward organizational changes the company could make to accommodate the designers' aspirations and repair the relationship. But note that the breach in the relationship—or, at least, its severity—had not been apparent to management until the designers threatened to leave *en masse*. Moreover, the reasons for the breach had not been clear to management or even to the designers themselves. They all thought it was about money, and it wasn't. It took an industrial psychologist to help them figure it out, but it was basically about the company giving them respect, a larger role, and greater opportunity to stretch their intellectual and professional capabilities.

FROM THE RAM PLAYBOOK

Implicit wins can make or break a relationship. Implicit wins have to do with intangible wins that aren't expressed because they're assumed by one or both parties. Although all wins should be explicit, some typically are not discussed.

For instance, most parties to a budding business relationship do not discuss matters of common courtesy or everyday forms of recognition. Yet they are important. Have you ever patronized a store regularly for several weeks or months and dealt with the same cashier who pretends that they've never seen you before? On the telephone, have you been kept on hold forever, listening to commercials for the company that is wasting your time? Have you ever done business with someone who courted you aggressively and then, after you made a deal, failed to communicate regularly?

Being treated well, being recognized, being in the loop, and not being taken for granted are wins that most stakeholders assume rather than discuss beforehand. After they're in a relationship, few stakeholders will call you because they feel underappreciated or your people lack enthusiasm. Instead, they will come to see your outfit as a poor place to do business. Then, when a more substantial loss occurs, it will be magnified by the feelings generated by small, day-to-day offenses, and the relationship will be that much more difficult to repair—if it can be repaired.

Consider implicit wins and be sure you deliver them—and communicate that you are delivering them. Many times employees, for example, need to be told about the benefits and other wins they're receiving. Some are unaware of them. Others discount their value. A number of companies explicitly tell employees, at meetings or through memos, the dollar value of their benefits. If you're supplying a win, the stakeholder should at least know about it.

Such mutinies are relatively rare. When they do occur, they are fueled by widespread resentment and anger. More often it is individual employees, customers, investors, and strategic partners who become disenchanted and, one by one, decide move on. That's preferable to mass defection, yet detecting dissatisfaction before things reach a boiling point—within an individual or a group—numbers among the key responsibilities of relationship owners. That requires continual monitoring. Formal periodic RAM assessments (discussed in Principle #10, "Get Rolling and Maintain Momentum") help the CRO, when there is one in place, and relationship owners to keep the RAM program progressing. Yet those formal periodic assessments can't take the place of ongoing monitoring.

Most of us have an innate sense of how we feel we're being treated in a relationship. However, we're less intuitive when it comes to the other party. Thus, to know where they stand, you must assess the balance of the wins, spoke out, and ask the other party how he feels about the way things are going. The opening of that conversation can be as straightforward as, "Here are the wins we're achieving, and here are the wins that we believe you're getting. How does this square with your point of view?" You must also notice and respond to signs of stakeholder dissatisfaction, which include …

1. Verbal and written complaints, which should be noted for their patterns and trends as well as for their content.

2. Even a slight unexplained uptick in employee turnover or customer defections.

3. Movement toward an alternative to your company, which indicates encroachment by a competitor or stakeholder dissatisfaction.

4. Fall-off in performance (among employees, suppliers, distributors, licensees, or strategic partners).

5. Fall-off in demonstrated interest (among job seekers, investors, the media, charities, and community groups).

6. Diminishing communication, particularly from contacts who usually do communicate.

7. Feelings of resentment, suspicion, or being taken for granted on your part.

Remember that you can never assume that the other party feels the way you do about the relationship, either positively or negatively. You have to learn how that party feels. When someone is dissatisfied or drifts away, find out why. Otherwise, you can't fix the problem. So, the first step is to find the problem. (We summarize step 2, fix what's broken, later in this chapter.)

STEP 1: FIND THE PROBLEM

The following questions will help you diagnose the problem in a business relationship:

1. Why do we believe the relationship is broken (lack of communication, unreturned phone calls, increase in complaints, threats to end the relationship)?

2. When did we first notice these symptoms? Who noticed them?

3. Who is the owner of the relationship? Who else has contact with the stakeholder?

4. Did anyone insult or offend anyone on the stakeholder's side? Has there been a disagreement lately?

5. Do we explicitly understand the wins for us in this relationship? What is the stakeholder's understanding of his wins?

6. Does the problem center on the basic business arrangement—the wins that the stakeholder expected to receive—or does it center on the conduct of the relationship (neglect, unintended offense, or lack of communication)?

7. What changes have occurred on either side in this relationship?

8. What is the touch schedule, in terms of type and frequency? Has the schedule been implemented? With what results? (This is one reason you need solid documentation of touches, their type, date and outcome, and the people involved.)

9. Was the relationship ever good? When was the relationship at its best?

10. What factors—business conditions, expected and delivered wins, personal relationships, and so on—characterized the relationship at its height? Can those factors be put in place again or somehow be re-created?

Note that the answer "We don't know" might be the correct one for some of these questions. That answer indicates a need for some research and communication. Understanding the problem before you try to fix it could entail coming right out and asking the stakeholder what's wrong.

WHAT'S THE SOLUTION?

Many people leave relationships rather than repair them. That might seem to be the easiest course of action, and, in a way, it is. Few people enjoy talking about the condition of a relationship, and, when they feel offended, most tend to see confrontation as the only option. Few people enjoy confrontation, so, rather than deal with that unpleasantness, most will leave the relationship. In addition, because the United States is something of a "throwaway" society, people are more likely to try to replace a relationship than to fix it.

RAM strategy brings a calmer, more reasoned approach to broken relationships. When something has gone wrong with a stakeholder, someone has to address it by proceeding with goodwill, communicating clearly and reasonably, reestablishing trust, and focusing on mutual wins. That someone might be the relationship owner, the CRO, if the company has one, or the entire contact team. The specific task faced depends on the stakeholder and on the nature and size of the problem identified. However, the following guidelines have helped us and our colleagues get relationships back on track.

THE NEED FOR SPEED

The principle says "When something breaks, fix it *fast*" for three reasons. First, acting quickly keeps resentment from building up on the stakeholder's side. Why allow time for attitudes to harden? Second, working to fix the problem fast shows that you value the relationship. Third, the sooner you fix the problem, the sooner you make the other party whole and limit the damage he suffers. Keep in mind that the situation could be relatively minor within the scope of your business, but quite important to the stakeholder.

Here's yet another way in which a company's investment in a CRO pays dividends. With a CRO in place, no one can say, "Gee, we didn't know who to call or what to do," or "I didn't have time to fix it, with everything else on my plate." The CRO is the resource and, for major relationships, "command central" for the repair squad. Every relationship owner must understand that at the first sight of a smoldering long-term problem or a sudden wildfire, they need to pick up the phone and call the CRO for strategic advice and tactical assistance.

QUICK FIXES

Essentially, there are two ways a relationship gets into trouble—quickly and slowly. A relationship can instantly implode on either a small scale (for instance, after a late delivery or minor oversight) or on a grand scale (as in a product-safety scare or the discovery of large amounts of missing money). Handled properly, an unexpected flare-up can be easier (though not necessarily cheaper) to address than long-term deterioration. The causes of sudden problems tend to be easily identified and readily addressable, while long-term decay often has multiple causes with complex emotional dimensions and fewer obvious remedies.

In either case, but especially in a fast-breaking situation, the first step is damage control. By that we mean damage to your reputation, to the other party, and to the relationship. This usually entails ...

- Accepting responsibility for your role in the situation.
- Apologizing for your role.
- Taking short-term measures to address the situation.

When you *accept responsibility* for your part in a foul-up, you garner goodwill, sympathy, and credibility. Conversely, failing to acknowledge your role could cast suspicion on you. For instance, Ford and Firestone would have done more to reassure the motoring public if they had each acknowledged that they had some role in the situation and that they were working to determine the extent of each company's responsibility.

Incidentally, parties that refuse to accept their share of the responsibility in a situation often resort to blaming others and finger-pointing. Finger-pointing begets finger-pointing, as Ford and Firestone demonstrated. Generally, when outfits try to make one another look bad, they both succeed. In contrast, when you acknowledge your role in creating a problem, you invite the other party to do the same.

Apologizing for your role comes after you acknowledge it. We all do things we wish we hadn't, yet too many of us can't say "I'm sorry." Some fear that it's a sign of weakness or believe their apology will be used against them. Others lack confidence in themselves or their associates. Actually, an apology is a sign of strength. People with confidence and people who trust others can admit their mistakes. The other party knows what you've done. When you apologize, they realize that you know it, too, and that you accept responsibility for it. This re-establishes trust and fosters faith in your willingness to do things differently in the future. On that note, the best apologies come with minimal explanation. "I'm sorry. I fouled up," followed by how you'll fix the situation or handle things the next time works far better than "I'm sorry, but …" with an explanation that says it really wasn't your fault.

Some people go a step further and apologize when there's genuine doubt about who's at fault or even when they're definitely not at fault. This technique defuses tense situations and enables both parties to move forward. People using the proactive apology correctly reason that it costs nothing, and if it allows someone to save face or get unstuck, it's worth it. Even if the other party doesn't acknowledge his role, he will appreciate the apology.

Apologizing is as easy as sincerely saying, "I apologize." Other helpful phrases include, "I'm afraid I misunderstood," "I should have been clearer," and "We overlooked that."

Short-term measures to remedy the situation can range from directly compensating the injured party to recalling possibly unsafe products, presenting plans to prevent future financial losses, or surrendering to the proper authorities.

FROM THE RAM PLAYBOOK

When you are the injured party, resist the urge to retaliate. You won't look good. You won't help the relationship. And you won't learn anything.

At SCG, we had a situation in which we failed to build enough co-ownership with a client. We left it all to the team of consultants on the project. One day, that project team decided they could do better for themselves by going out on their own and using that client relationship as the foundation for starting their own firm. When the project was almost 50 percent complete, the consultants told the client that they were leaving SCG to start their own firm, and that they could deliver the same work at a lower rate. The client saw the economic benefit of this and accepted the offer. (Obviously, we had failed to see the warning signs of our deteriorating relationship with a key group of employees.)

Under the circumstances, we felt no need to apologize to anyone, but we also saw no use in retaliating. We might have *felt* like giving the client a piece of our mind or threatening our project team with legal action. However, retaliating wasn't going to save the relationship.

Instead, we examined our role in the situation. We hadn't built enough multilevel links into the client or employee relationship. We didn't have a noncompete/nonsolicitation agreement that would rein in employees who faced these temptations, nor did we have a clause in our contract with the client that prevented this. Therefore, we redoubled our RAM efforts and asked our staff to help us develop a fair noncompete/nonsolicitation agreement. We also added a protective clause to our client contract. Going forward, we still did a lot of work for this client in other areas, and we were protected from this sort of thing happening again.

The relationship with our former employees was initially broken, and professional tension partially fueled by market competition remained for a while. A couple years ago, however, the project team that had left with our client approached us for some business advice. We sat down to lunch with them and gave them a few pointers because we had seen our role in the situation, had prevented similar incidents from occurring, and saw no point in having an adversarial relationship with them.

That last statement raises an issue. When an employee does something illegal that affects stakeholders, senior management must accept responsibility for having the person on staff and promptly issue an apology. The employee must be reprimanded and, if appropriate, terminated, suspended, or directed to make restitution as soon as possible. Then management must develop a way of preventing similar occurrences in the future.

STRUCTURAL REPAIRS

When a relationship has deteriorated over time, the approach to fixing it might differ from those applied to suddenly sticky situations. These relationships typically delivered mutual wins in the past but then faded away over time due to changes in personnel, organizational goals, or business conditions. Infrequent communication, or no communication, characterizes almost all faded relationships.

If such a relationship represents a potentially valuable asset, try a RAM revival—a two-step process. In the first step, the relationship owner, other contact people, and, if there's one on board, the CRO should meet and review the history of the relationship. Pull any relevant records and documentation, and try to understand when and why the relationship was at its peak, and when and how the relationship deteriorated. Mentally re-create the best days of the relationship with that stakeholder or group of stakeholders. Recall the patterns of contact; the people involved; the things both sides were doing; and the goals, success factors, and risks that generated the wins. Review the operational issues of that time and the overall business conditions. Then try to trace the changes in the relationship.

The second step in a RAM revival is to take a fresh approach to defining potential wins—what are the current goals, success factors, and risks each party faces?—and use the results to create a new set of expectations. We're not saying that the original wins and expectations can't play a role in the revival, but trying to resurrect them might invoke a been-there-done-that response. New wins and expectations will probably do more to reinvigorate a relationship. So might a new approach to the stakeholder.

For instance, an economic forecasting outfit we know of conducted a RAM revival. The firm had once enjoyed superb relationships with Fortune 500 clients, who relied on economic data in their strategic-planning processes. Strategic planning was in its heyday, and large staffs of analysts worked on one-, three-, and five-year plans for the corporation as a whole and for individual divisions. They used reams of economic data in creating models of alternative scenarios and projecting performance under varying conditions. However, those relationships faded when centralized, long-term strategic planning fell out of favor, clients downsized their planning functions, and turnover on both sides weakened the personal links between the company and its clients. Ideally, the firm would have wanted to return to the earlier days of the relationship. The company realized that this was impossible, yet it decided to try a revival.

To do this, the forecasting firm shifted its focus to financial managers. These managers had superseded strategic planners at those client companies and had a need for economic information. To pursue them, the firm leveraged the relationships that a sister company, which sold investment research, had built with financial managers. The firm also developed simplified economic models for the finance function and new products to help manage international risks, which had grown in importance. They set up new pricing structures and new delivery mechanisms, including a Web site. This gave the firm a totally fresh approach to the Fortune 500, which did revive a number of relationships.

Approaching the stakeholder with a new framework for the relationship and a new set of wins based on current goals, success factors, and risks will shift the point of view from the past to the future. Knowing what made the relationship work in the first place (if it did, that is—you can't revive what was never alive) and knowing what has changed can help you develop a new framework and new wins.

WHAT IF YOU'RE ON THE OUTS?

If a relationship has been dormant, rather than broken, a direct approach based on new wins will probably reopen the lines of communication and start renewing the relationship. But if the stakeholder parted in anger or there are frosty feelings in the air, you might have to repair past damage before working on the future. Some stakeholders might not want to hash over past hurts. However, pretending that nothing bad occurred might offend an offended stakeholder even further. ("So he calls up acting like nothing happened. If he thinks I'm doing business with him again, he's nuts.")

There are several revival tactics to try in such situations. Each of them should be used in a spirit of what management consultant Emmett Murphy calls "strategic humility." With strategic humility, you put your feelings aside for the good of your organization. The saying "Nothing ventured, nothing gained" also applies. A decent, well-intentioned attempt to revive a dormant relationship can't make matters much worse, while the upside potential is a new start for both parties.

An apology from you could be in order—even if you feel that you don't owe one to anybody. (That's strategic humility!) Getting a third party whom you both trust to break the ice or broker a peace can guide both parties to a renewed relationship. This is particularly true if that third party would like to see you together again. Letting the other party suggest ways to fix the relationship will point to what that party sees as fair and signal that you're willing to play ball. The other party also will gain a sense of control.

Don't expect an immediate revival. It takes time to rebuild a dormant, damaged relationship. Don't expect someone you've hurt—or even someone who feels hurt when you believe he shouldn't—to come around overnight. While the stakeholder is working things through for himself, use well-chosen, relatively light touches to renew regular contact. Shared experiences and confidences and the search for mutual wins can rebuild relationships in the same ways that they build them in the first place. It's up to you to create situations in which that can happen.

Renewing a worthwhile relationship is always worth the effort. You have some positive (in addition to the negative) history and mutual knowledge to use as a foundation. On that foundation, you can establish new expectations and new wins and a game plan for creating them.

WHEN YOU'RE ON THE LOSING SIDE

When you feel offended in a relationship or believe that the balance of wins has tilted against you, you must address the situation. Your first impulse could be to end the association. Although that might be the best course of action, don't be too quick to pursue it. Often that impulse arises from a desire to avoid the confrontation that might be needed to set things right.

If you're providing the wins that you agreed to provide but the other party is not delivering, you need to talk. Lose-win relationships are untenable. The relationship owner must review the original expected wins and the history of the wins actually achieved. Then he must sit down and conduct a similar review with the stakeholder and reach agreement regarding the variance between expectations and performance.

In implementing RAM, sometimes you have to be tough. Call it the RAM admonition. Correcting misunderstandings, criticizing performance, and insisting that your wins be delivered are part of doing business. RAM is certainly not about looking the other way while people take advantage of you. It is about developing shared value and about keeping all parties focused on that goal.

KNOWING WHEN TO QUIT

Nothing in this chapter should be taken to mean that every relationship can be saved or is worth saving. Some *can't* be saved, and some *aren't* worth saving. When the wins are all on the stakeholder's side and there's no way to change that, feel free to continue a personal relationship, if there is one, but the business relationship must end. It's not fair to the company or to other stakeholders to continue in a one-sided situation.

Why do companies or businesspeople stay in one-sided relationships? In the absence of information and analysis, they might not realize how one-sided some of them can be. Or, they might know it and continue out of habit, tradition, fear of confrontation, or just plain laziness. Ending a business arrangement and replacing a stakeholder are chores most of us would rather not undertake.

Don't underestimate the costs of continuing a poor relationship. These costs, which vary according to the situation and the stakeholder, include forgone opportunities to link up with better stakeholders and the stress that bad relationships put on other parties. Such costs can be considerable. For example, although this happens less often than in the past, many managers still tolerate poorly performing employees. They can't hack the termination process, or they fear the bad feelings and legal action that firing someone can generate. Yet that poorly performing employee takes up a slot and a salary that could be given to one who would pull his weight. Other employees have to pick up the slacker's slack, which hurts morale and leads some to lower their standards.

Similarly, relationships with suppliers, strategic partners, licensees, or independent distributors who agree to deliver wins and then fail to must be fixed or ended quickly. They take up energy that could be better applied to putting productive stakeholders in those roles. Relationships must be severed immediately with any stakeholder who betrays you (or betrays anyone else, for that matter), who demonstrates a lack of ethics, or who engages in or asks you to engage in illegal activity. Knowing when to quit a bad relationship saves resources and promotes a better night's sleep.

Even customer relationships should be ended when the wins are out of whack. But it must be done gracefully. Years ago, a study revealed that a major New York bank was losing money on checking accounts with average balances of under roughly $1,000. Having decided that this was not a win, the bank sent these customers letters directing them to close their accounts within 90 days. The ensuing firestorm of negative publicity, which cited every family's need for a checking account and the implicit bias against poorer customers, was so bad that the bank withdrew the directive.

It can be preferable to allow stakeholders to leave through attrition. For instance, large credit card companies have customer retention units. Customers who call to close their accounts are referred to these units, where specially trained account reps are authorized to take measures to save the relationship. The reps can renegotiate interest rates and finance charges, and present payment options and services that the customer might not have known about. However, these retention units do not attempt to save unprofitable accounts. If the computer shows that customer rarely uses the card, never carries balances, or pays erratically, the rep cheerfully allows him to cut up his card.

Although some bad relationships can be allowed to trail off, it's best to end any that you can explicitly, quickly, and with a brief, kindly worded explanation or excuse. There's little point in believing that there's a relationship where none exists, yet the association should be ended, as the Italians say, *senza rancore,* without rancor, without bad feelings. Remember, former stakeholders can change—some return to solid stakeholder status—and it never pays to have anyone embittered about having done business with you.

STEP 2: FIX WHAT'S BROKEN

When you have identified the problem in a valuable relationship, one or more of the following measures, chosen according to the problem that needs to be fixed, will usually enable you to get the relationship back on track.

BEFORE APPROACHING THE STAKEHOLDER

1. Develop a clear understanding of your company's version of the situation.

2. Decide whether to approach the stakeholder or to implement the fix proactively.

3. If it's better to approach the stakeholder, decide who on your side is best positioned to do that (or consider a mutually trusted third party).

4. Identify who on the stakeholder's side would be the best person, or best people, to approach.

5. Decide whether you owe the stakeholder an apology (also consider apologizing even if you don't owe one).

6. If the wins are unbalanced, examine ways of rebalancing them before you approach the stakeholder.

7. If an operational error created the difficulty in the relationship, correct it and advise the stakeholder that it has been corrected.

8. Examine the agreed-upon wins and record of delivery on the wins in order to determine: Are all the wins explicit? Are they understood by each side? Does each side agree that the wins, as defined, are fair? (Sometimes people agree to a deal and later decide that they short-changed themselves and feel resentment even though you are delivering their wins.)

WITH THE STAKEHOLDER

1. Explicitly state that the relationship is important to you and your entity, and that you want to get things back on track.

2. Apologize and accept responsibility for the problem—or, if you're not responsible, simply apologize for not initiating this discussion earlier, if it would help move things forward.

3. Review the wins and expectations, and make sure you are both in agreement. If it will help clarify things, review the history of the wins achieved.

4. If appropriate, explain to the stakeholder that you've made every effort to ensure that the error or offense doesn't happen again.

5. Ask the stakeholder what he feels would be a fair solution.

6. If appropriate, provide a compensatory win, such as a discount, refund, or replacement merchandise.

7. Close by stating that you value the relationship and that you look forward to working together for a long time to come.

8. Give it time, especially if the repair involves rebuilding trust.

9. Ask the stakeholder to describe the relationship in detail a year down the road, if everything is going well in the relationship.

10. Try a RAM revival on dormant but potentially valuable relationships.

PUTTING RELATIONSHIPS ON THE COMEBACK TRAIL

Before writing off an asset on the balance sheet, such as a past-due account, an aging machine, or an unused building, management will consciously decide its fate. Often the company will rehabilitate the asset or, if it is to be disposed of, attempt to realize the greatest possible value on it. Nevertheless, companies regularly abandon relationship assets without a thought about their true value or any attempt to repair them. Not fixing a relationship that has deteriorated is a decision to write it off. We believe that, at the least, such a decision should be made consciously. In most cases, reasonable steps should be taken to put a derailed relationship back on track. This means that you must know the value of the relationship to the company (which we examine in Principle #11, "Maximize the Long-Term Value of Relationships") and employ the right means of fixing what's broken.

It's worth the effort. As with so many RAM practices, few companies take the trouble to do this consistently. Therefore, repairing relationships or seeing them though rough patches will confer competitive advantage on companies that do. Most relationships grow in value over time, so they're worth holding on to from that standpoint.

Almost every enduring relationship—business or personal—will occasionally hit bumpy spots. Many will also experience a full-blown crisis. To build long-term relationships, you can't define a good relationship as one with no difficulties, but rather as one in which both stakeholders work to resolve difficulties equitably.

POST-GAME WRAP-UP

- It's easier to fix relationships than most businesspeople think, yet it does take effort to discover what's wrong and then to fix it. Communication within the company and with the stakeholder represents the main tool for finding and fixing the problem.
- Monitoring stakeholders, as individuals and as groups, constitutes an ongoing activity for the CRO, relationship owners, and everyone on the contact team.
- The faster you repair a suddenly damaged relationship, the better. To do so, accept your part in the matter, apologize, and suggest and implement remedies.
- To revive a dormant relationship or one damaged long ago, review the history and identify both when and why it was at its peak, and when and how it deteriorated. Then develop new wins based on current realities.
- When you are on the losing end, you must methodically review the expected wins on each side and compare them with the achieved wins on each side. Then have a serious discussion with the stakeholder. If the stakeholder will not be reasonable, you might have a permanently broken relationship.
- Some relationships must be ended. Nonperformers take up space, cause aggravation, and exact a price from the company. People who betray others or lack ethics are worse still.
- Virtually all relationships go through difficulties. Those difficulties don't mean that the relationship should be discarded, but that it needs repairs.

PRINCIPLE #10:

GET ROLLING AND MAINTAIN MOMENTUM

You must have a sound basic plan to have any chance of success, but it is the individual team members who must execute the plan. Many mountaineering expeditions—or, for that matter, the fate of nations—have failed because individuals have been given the wrong job or have failed to work together as a team.

—*From* Everest the Hard Way, *by Chris Bonington*

In other words, for any endeavor to succeed, the right people with the right plan must work together on the right things. RAM provides an overall philosophy, a general approach, specific guidelines, and practical tools for developing and employing win-centric relationships to achieve success. This book has also provided examples of RAM strategy in action from our business experience, and cited positive and negative examples from the business press and our general knowledge of business. Now it's time to implement the program. This principle provides ways and means of starting and maintaining a RAM effort in a company, a department, a small business, or in your own career.

As we have noted, RAM is a simple concept. But that doesn't mean it is effortless. The well-known formula for losing weight and getting in shape—proper diet and regular exercise—is also simple, but it takes sustained effort for it to yield results. Similarly, RAM requires planning, performance, and perseverance.

Implementing RAM involves changes in your thinking and behavior in business relationships. Those relationships—the raw material you need to put RAM into practice—are all around you, and that's both a positive and a negative. On the positive side, because you already have relationships and are regularly being exposed to potential new ones, RAM does not involve a massive investment in materials or equipment. You literally can get started with a desk, a phone, a pen and paper, and the head on your shoulders. On the negative side, however, you face the inertia of habitual ways of thinking and behaving in your relationships. To get RAM rolling, you must first overcome that inertia.

KICKING OFF A RAM PROGRAM

Powerful forces in ourselves and in our organizations resist change. After all, it is far easier not to do something than it is to do it. Excuses for the status quo abound: We're not doing badly, we're ahead of the competition, people already enjoy doing business with us, we're too busy as it is. Therefore, the RAM Sell—selling yourself and your colleagues on the benefits of RAM—constitutes an early step in implementation. Once the benefits to you or your company are on the table, you have justification and motivation for inaugurating a RAM program.

THE RAM SELL

By now you know the general benefits of RAM: It enables a person, department, or company to achieve goals, enhance success factors, and mitigate risks. It helps you identify and cultivate relationships with people who can help you succeed. It makes people stakeholders in each other's success. It generates long-term relationships that grow in value over time. It creates closer, more personal relationships, which make a business run more smoothly and make doing business more fun. Yet these benefits, as attractive as they are, are too general to galvanize an organization, or even most individuals, into action. And that's really good news for those who do take action.

The RAM Sell relates the benefits of RAM to a specific person or entity by revealing the gap between current and potential performance. It also shows the costs and benefits of RAM compared with other, more traditional methods of getting things done. We mentioned gap analysis and cost-benefit analysis in Principle #2, "Develop a Game Plan." Now we examine their role in RAM more closely.

GAP ANALYSIS AND COST-BENEFIT ANALYSIS

Gap analysis reveals the difference between your current set of relationship assets and the set that you actually need. It also measures the distance between the performance of your current relationship assets and your desired performance—which could be attained with those assets plus additional ones, all being aggressively managed. To measure the gaps, take each goal, success factor, and risk, and then examine your Relationship Web (or your department's or company's web). Next, take some time to identify which current relationships could help you achieve the goals, enhance the success factors, and mitigate the risks. Then look beyond the Relationship Web and determine what relationships you would need to develop to achieve all your goals, enhance all success factors, and mitigate all risks. On the performance side, you are also measuring the added value and contribution you could extract from current relationships. There is *always* unmined gold in existing relationships before RAM is initiated.

For instance, suppose you've identified a new, fast-growing, high-potential market for your company's products or services. Can you reach that market effectively with your current relationships? How would those relationships have to be modified to reach that market? Which completely new relationships would enable you to reach that market? For instance, who currently sells to them? What type of salespeople seem to succeed in that new market? Are distributors with products that complement yours already calling on companies in that market? Are there ways—through certain media or endorsements, for example—that you could get companies in that new market to come to you or have greater trust in you when you come calling? Identify everyone who might help you if you had a relationship with them. (This is where a diligent cultivation effort really pays off. The more relationships you have cultivated with potential stakeholders, the larger the base that you can draw from.)

When you know which of your current relationships can help you and which new ones you need, you can gauge the gap between your current Relationship Web and your ideal one. Be sure, however, not to underestimate those current relationships. For each existing stakeholder, you must answer the question: What is the gap between the current mutual wins we are both achieving and those we could achieve?

A good measure of the justification and motivation for RAM comes from seeing the gap between the current relationship set and the set you need. When you realize that closing that gap, even partially, will translate to goals achieved, success factors enhanced, and risks mitigated—that is, to faster growth, greater profits, higher quality, smoother operations, and greater security—then you can make the case for a RAM program.

Cost-benefit analysis heightens motivation even further by defining the benefits more precisely and by demonstrating the cost-effectiveness of RAM in comparison with other methods of accomplishing the same things. Here's how this helps with the RAM Sell: When you demonstrate the difference between the current and ideal sets of relationship assets, some people might respond, "There's a gap. So what?"

The answer might be, "So this: If by developing a good relationship with the right vendor, we meet one otherwise unreachable prospect in this new market a week, that's 50 a year. If we close one in eight of them, which is our average close rate, that's six new engagements a year. At our average fee of $Y per project, that translates to $X of incremental revenue a year. And we'll do this with minimal incremental expenditures. The major costs will be the expense of developing the relationship with the right vendor—mainly phone calls, lunches, and a bit of travel—and, of course, the expense of the sales calls themselves. And we'll incur no advertising, direct mail, or telemarketing expenses on those sales."

FROM THE RAM PLAYBOOK

A Manhattan advertising agency submitted a large job to a major commercial printer. The job, for the agency's largest financial services client, was an insert going into hundreds of thousands of Sunday newspapers.

In the printing business, the customer, not the printer, is responsible for typos or other errors in the text. Thus, most press operators simply set up the job on their press and then let it run. The pressman on this job, however, first took a good look at the insert. When he did, he saw the word "pubic" in the text. This being a financial services piece, the pressman instantly realized that the word should be "public." He telephoned the folks at the ad agency, who corrected the error and resubmitted the job a few hours later.

The next day, the ad agency's creative director messengered a Rolex watch to the press operator, along with a letter of thanks.

Now, we don't know whether the pressman always looks over his jobs or, in this case, gave the insert special attention because he liked the people at the agency or because he had received tickets to a ballgame for catching an error in the past.

But we can be pretty sure of a few things: The pressman likes his Rolex—and loves to tell his co-workers how he got it. In the future, he'll keep a sharp eye out for typos on that ad agency's jobs—and probably on other jobs, too. His co-workers might start looking more closely at the jobs they run, as well. The press operator's boss must surely see his relationship with that pressman as a valuable asset. And, not incidentally, the ad agency probably won't be changing commercial printers anytime soon. Wins all over the place.

And the cost of the Rolex? Nothing, really, considering the win the pressman delivered.

As part of its employee recruitment effort, Adjoined Technologies spent $20 apiece to have "care packages" delivered to 40 IT majors who were studying for their final exams at a nearby university. The packages included Starbucks coffee, Power Bars, snack foods, and such. Cost-benefit analysis told Adjoined that $800 spent on a memorable win for 40 hand-picked potential candidates is a bargain compared with scatter-shot advertisements in the Sunday paper for hundreds of dollars each or recruiter's fees of $2,000 to $3,000 per hire. Moreover, providing that win got the relationship between the company and the candidate off to a beautiful start. Adjoined did not offer a position to everyone in that group of 40, but every candidate who was extended an offer accepted it.

The incredible cost-effectiveness of RAM strategy really comes to light when it's compared with "traditional" methods of reaching the same goals. RAM cannot solve every problem, but on those it can address, it will usually blow away other methods on a cost-benefit basis. Most RAM strategies entail minimal out-of-pocket expenses—phone calls, networking, lunches, socializing, business entertaining, some travel, and small but thoughtful proactive wins, such as those "care packages" for the students facing their finals. Aside from such expenses, most RAM strategies mainly require an investment of brainpower, creativity, and interpersonal energy rather than large sums of money.

RAM ASSESSMENT

An in-depth assessment of existing stakeholder relationships is necessary before initiating a RAM program. Then, after a RAM program is implemented, relationships must be assessed on a regular basis, with a frequency appropriate to the nature and importance of the relationship—and whenever a problem or change arises. These assessments—that is, the initial and the ongoing—are similar, although they obviously occur under different circumstances. What exactly is being assessed? The condition of the company's (or department's or person's) relationships, the balance of the wins on both sides, the risks to the relationship, and the value—including the unmined value—in the relationship. The results of an assessment feed into the plan for initiating RAM or for moving an existing RAM program forward.

To work well, a RAM assessment (particularly the initial assessment) must be conducted in a spirit of learning, improving, and looking to the future. If people now responsible for stakeholder relationships see the process as an investigation into their past performance, they'll become defensive. That would get things off on the wrong foot and perhaps scuttle the entire effort.

The following questions (applicable at the level of the relationship between the entities and between the individuals within the entities) should be applied to each identifiable stakeholder relationship in the various stakeholder groups:

1. What wins are we currently deriving from this relationship?
2. What wins is the stakeholder deriving from the relationship?
3. What is the balance of wins—current, historical, and projected?
4. Who is the owner of the relationship? Who else has regular contact?
5. What is the touch schedule? Is it being maintained?
6. What is the plan to realize the wins we are now pursuing?
7. What unmined wins might reside in this relationship, on both sides?
8. Are we at risk of losing this relationship if our key contact, or the stakeholder's key contact, leaves?
9. What RAM insurance (discussed in a later section) do we have in place? How could we add more insurance on major relationships?
10. What is the overall condition of the relationship with this stakeholder?
11. What is the balance of the wins in this entire stakeholder group?
12. What is the condition of our relationship with this stakeholder group?

Answers to these questions should be written down separately by each person conducting the assessment and then compared and reconciled into a single assessment for the stakeholder. Of course, these questions can and should be enhanced with others developed for the specific entity or individual.

Whenever possible, try to quantify the wins (money saved or earned on each side of the relationship, or the number of tangible wins, such as new accounts or new products developed). It's also a good idea to capture any quantifiable indicators of the relationship's condition (number of stakeholders lost or stakeholder complaints). For non-quantifiable aspects, it's particularly important that a few people familiar with the relationship make the assessment.

The deliverable in this process would be a profile or fact sheet on each relationship for use by the CRO and other senior managers and the relationship owners. The whole assessment process should give management the information and motivation to plan and execute a formal RAM program, if there isn't one already in place.

After a program is in place, a quarterly RAM assessment of this type will keep the RAM team members aware of the condition of their relationships. It will also enable them to enhance and improve the relationship; take corrective action when necessary; and, in the subsequent assessment, judge how effective the program was in the previous quarter. This iterative process keeps the team organized and on a learning curve. Note, however, that because relationships can change so quickly, a company needs to think in terms of constant, ongoing informal assessment as well, to detect changes and adjust to their impact as soon as possible.

The outcome of the assessment must be a clear, agreed-upon understanding of the state of each relationship. The next step would be a plan for improving the relationship by adjusting the type or schedule of touches, developing new wins with the stakeholder, or taking other steps to strengthen the bond, build trust, and improve the value on both sides.

RAM PLAN

When you are ready to move forward, implementing the plan comprises the following steps. We've covered them earlier, so we'll quickly review them here:

- Identify your goals, success factors, and risks—the wins you want to achieve.

- Identify all your stakeholder groups and every stakeholder and potential stakeholder within each group.

- Take each goal, success factor, and risk, and survey your current and ideal Relationship Web to assess how each stakeholder could help you achieve that win.

- Define potential wins for each stakeholder and potential stakeholder, on the basis of your knowledge of them and on the basis of research by spoking out and asking them.

- Assign or confirm an owner for every relationship, if you have not already done so.

- Identify individuals to contact at every entity, if you haven't done so. Create contact schedules as well as individual plans at the micro level to build the relationship, discover interests, define wins more precisely, and establish a bond.

- Implement the plan and maintain the relationship. Conduct regular assessments and adjust the plan accordingly.

The preceding are the broad elements of a RAM plan, which an entity or individual will customize as necessary. The discipline of formulating and following a plan raises RAM to the level of a true strategic effort, which it must be to take the company where it needs to go. Without a written plan that is discussed and shared, you will have only some new ideas and a few new tools for doing things differently in your business relationships. That is not a RAM program.

RAM INSURANCE

Suppose you are the CEO of a mid-size company and into your office bursts your head of sales, filled with excitement. Your star salesperson on the West Coast has been cultivating a relationship with Acme Company for almost two years, and it has finally paid off. Acme is going to purchase $1.8 million worth of your product over the next two years.

The RAM-savvy CEO would say, "This is great, but … what if our salesperson leaves us? What if he leaves for a competitor? Is the relationship truly between our two companies? Or is it between our salesperson and the buyer at Acme? What if the buyer leaves?" If the answer to these questions is "I don't know," or worse, then there is no RAM insurance and the company has to get some in place quickly.

Most business insurance is designed to compensate the insured if disaster strikes. It indemnifies the company against the financial losses associated with the event. Fire insurance pays for the building that was destroyed, but it doesn't prevent fires. Liability insurance compensates people who are injured, but it doesn't prevent injuries. In contrast, RAM insurance aims to prevent a loss rather than compensate for it. As assets, relationships must be protected, primarily against loss. If they are damaged, there are methods for repairing them (as discussed in Principle #9, "When Something Breaks, Fix It Fast"). But if they are lost, they might be gone forever and there's really no way to compensate a company for that. Therefore, RAM insurance aims to prevent the loss of a relationship.

RAM insurance consists of a number of tools, many of which are currently in use to some degree in business. A company has RAM insurance on a relationship when it actively employs as many of these tools as possible to reduce the risk of losing that relationship.

FIVE FORMS OF RAM INSURANCE

1. **Multiple links.** The greater the number of links and connections there are between people on both sides of the relationship, the greater the chance that the relationship between the entities will survive if a serious problem arises or if someone on either side leaves. Multiple links offer some protection against employees taking a customer relationship with them when they resign. These

links also strengthen the relationship in general—and the stronger the relationship, the less chance that you'll lose it for whatever reason.

As detailed in Principle #3, "Create Ownership for Relationships," a company must work at establishing multiple links. Every person with stakeholder contact must have a sense of ownership for the relationship. Responsiveness, flexibility, knowledge of the stakeholder, and a system of keeping information accessible all enable a contact team to work smoothly. We mentioned how at Burger King, our policy of working to fulfill every stakeholder request promptly, regardless of where it originated, enabled us to build multiple links and make our client, the IT function, look good. With that kind of effort, people in many areas of the stakeholder entity can be drawn into the relationship.

When relationships require multiple links because of their size and importance, they also require first-rate coordination of the relationship management team. As we also said in Principle #3, every relationship requires one owner and, ideally, the company has a chief relationship officer in place. It is up to the relationship owner and the CRO to ensure that anyone in regular contact with the stakeholder entity is communicating with one voice and working on specific areas of responsibility.

2. **Written agreements and contracts.** Every company needs written agreements and legal contracts, including contracts with suppliers and strategic partners; service agreements with customers and suppliers; employment contracts for key employees; written agreements with independent contractors; and, of course, noncompete and nonsolicitation agreements (where enforceable) for any employee with knowledge of proprietary processes or the ability to "kidnap" customers. Pursuing legal recourse to enforce a contract obviously won't put a relationship back on track, but the existence of legal recourse provides some protection.

To prevent contracts and legal issues from tainting or sinking a relationship, use contracts that are "deal makers" rather than "deal breakers"—contracts that are win-win rather than win-lose. Such contracts offer equal protection, recourse, and rewards for both parties. This calls for an attorney who understands your business philosophy and who can take a "we'll-find-a-way" approach to making deals happen.

3. **Making stakeholders part of the business.** Stakeholders perceive a real stake in your success when you treat them as part of the business. Invite key customers and suppliers to see your operation and meet the people behind the scenes. Solicit their ideas for improvement. Get their thoughts on product and process improvements. Learn how you can truly become easier to do business with. Customer councils and supplier councils represent useful formal vehicles for doing these things. Share your plans (to a prudent extent) with stakeholders, including investors, lenders, and the community. Set up three-way wins, for instance, by sharing media exposure with stakeholders who can benefit from it. Always work to develop personal relationships in the context of business. Most people find it far harder to take advantage of someone they know as a person rather than only as a business associate.

4. **High switching costs.** As noted in the next chapter, in many industries customers incur high switching costs when they change suppliers—the expense of finding, evaluating, and developing a relationship with a new supplier, and the cost of changes to processes, equipment, and even other relationships. On one level, the more operational links you build between you and your stakeholders (customers, suppliers, and strategic partners) the harder it becomes for them (and you!) to end the relationship. Electronic data interchange (EDI) is a good example. When a computer-to-computer ordering, invoicing, and payment system exists between two companies, it becomes easier for them to do business. That,

in effect, creates a barrier to switching suppliers. When a financial institution provides payroll, checking, and international accounts, plus cash management and foreign exchange services, it has made changing banks that much more difficult.

One caveat: Build these links gradually as the relationship grows, or they could keep a new stakeholder from entering the relationship. For instance, they initially might not want to change their systems if that is a must for doing business with you. However, they might well do so after they know you and trust you.

5. **Solid maintenance.** The fundamental RAM technique, which provides a measure of insurance because so few companies do it consistently or well enough, remains solid, day-to-day maintenance. Have a good relationship owner and support him. Have a schedule of touches and stick with it. Always know the current balance of wins, and when it tilts too much in either direction, redress that balance. If your stakeholders trust you to search out and deliver genuine wins to them, they'll have very little desire to change their status vis-à-vis your company.

As you know, you are going to lose some stakeholders, including the occasional important, long-standing relationship. The only hope of winning any such stakeholder back rests in continuing to do the best job you can of running your business and handling that leave-taking with good manners and grace. Find out why the stakeholder wants to leave. Point out the benefits of staying (provided that you want him to, of course) and try to counter any competing offer, if you feel comfortable doing so. But recognize that when a stakeholder believes it's time to go, he will go. There's no point in trying to keep someone who wants to leave, but remember that stakeholders will often return when they find the grass no greener elsewhere.

Finally, if you're dealing with a stakeholder who practices a "burn and retreat" approach, the sooner you're rid of him, the better.

There will be fewer acres of scorched earth in your backyard, and the stakeholder can move on until he eventually runs out of fields to burn.

RAM MAINTENANCE

Much of the actual, ongoing work of implementing RAM comes down to actively maintaining relationships rather than letting them bounce along on their own. Maintenance consists of a series of actions you take to protect and improve your relationship assets.

A relationship requires maintenance, just as tangible assets such as vehicles and equipment do. And as with maintaining tangible assets, maintaining relationships might seem to be more work than not maintaining them, particularly if you're not in the habit of doing so. RAM maintenance does involve more front-end work than the myopic, reactive approach that most companies take toward most stakeholders. The net benefit and savings, though, accrue at the back end when you find yourself fighting fewer fires, hitting fewer points of friction, and sweeping up fewer pieces of broken relationships. Those benefits are in addition to all that the company gains in the form of more and larger wins.

The key maintenance activities are these:

- Developing ways of keeping in touch and building the relationship
- Determining the touch frequency and implementing the contact schedule
- Defining and delivering wins consistently
- Resolving issues as they arise
- Adjusting the plan iteratively and, whenever possible, involving the stakeholder in the adjustment effort

If you are using RAM properly, over time you will have relationships at every stage of development, from the early cultivation to the long-standing stage. Each of these five maintenance activities applies in some way to relationships at every stage. Also, each activity is the responsibility of the relationship owner. Relationship owners may delegate portions of these tasks, but they retain the responsibility for maintaining the relationships in their portfolios. We've already covered these activities in depth in earlier principles, so here we quickly place them in the context of a total maintenance effort.

Develop ways of keeping in touch: When you take steps to build a relationship, a good portion of those steps must be specific to the stakeholder. Yes, you should send them your quarterly newsletter, but that sort of "standard touch" is not enough. To create a bond and grow the relationship, the touches must be personal. You must learn what the stakeholder's interests are and, whenever possible, relate the touches and the relationship-building events to those interests.

This takes effort and planning. You must learn what events and pastimes your stakeholders enjoy and then extend invitations to those events and pastimes. If a stakeholder likes golf, get her out on a golf course. If she likes fishing, go fishing. Send magazine and newspaper clippings germane to her business and job function.

At the outset in a relationship, most touches can be "standard." Almost everyone enjoys an occasional evening at a ballgame or an art exhibit. They understand that the real goal is to get to know one another anyway. But as you get to know the stakeholder as a person, the touches and relationship-building occasions had better reflect the fact that you are getting to know them. You don't want them wondering why you keep inviting them to Japanese restaurants when you/they dislike sushi.

The more thought you give to your touches, the more thoughtful they will be.

Use a touch schedule: The touch schedule lies at the heart of RAM maintenance. Without RAM, most people try to track their touches in their heads and judge frequency by the seat of their pants. (The exception would be salespeople, who usually track calls on customers and prospects more carefully.) In-the-head and seat-of-the-pants might work for scheduling the relatively few people you might already be dealing with regularly. Those methods will definitely not work in a full-scale cultivation effort.

Maintenance of any kind, and especially preventive maintenance, must be done on a schedule. Think of it this way: If you don't have a written or computerized touch schedule, complete with a check-off or tracking system, then you don't have a maintenance program.

It's worth noting again that you should not reject this method of developing relationships as being "mechanical" or "calculated." If it seems mechanical, don't worry. You need a mechanism to keep dozens or hundreds or thousands of contacts organized. If it seems calculated, don't worry about that, either. Except in rare instances of pure luck, success is always the result of careful planning and diligent execution.

Define and deliver wins: The only thing to emphasize on this subject is that the best way to define wins is with the stakeholder. You can figure out wins for the stakeholder all day long, but, sooner or later (preferably sooner), you must sit down together and do business. Creating wins is a joint activity: "Here are the wins I'd like to achieve. Here are the ones I think you can achieve. What do you think?" Then you must deliver the wins, on time, as promised, and in good condition. "All hat and no cattle" will not maintain or sustain a relationship.

Resolve issues as they arise: Again, when something breaks, fix it fast. When a relationship gets off track or an operational problem occurs or the wins tilt too much toward either side, develop a provisional solution, pick up the phone, talk about it with the stakeholder, and get it resolved. Remember also that it's easier to fix relationships than most people realize.

Adjust the plan: Relationships are constantly changing. Even if a relationship could stand still, the environment around it is changing so fast that change will be thrust upon it. That means that the plan you had in place for the stakeholder yesterday—the type and frequency of touches, the wins you defined for one another, and the priority of the relationship (which we take up in the next principle)—might be outdated today.

Sudden change aside, any plan of any kind requires periodic review to ascertain that it is being executed properly, that it is achieving its objectives, and that it is being adjusted as needed. Every relationship, and every relationship management effort, is a work in progress. Implementing RAM is therefore an iterative process of planning execution-evaluation-planning-execution-evaluation, and so on.

BEING SYSTEMATIC

For RAM to become fully integrated into a company's infrastructure and to be as efficient and effective as possible, systems support at some level is necessary. A true RAM effort, particularly in a large company, requires and generates a lot of information that must be captured, tracked, and periodically reviewed. This includes stakeholder information; touch schedules; records of touches and their type, date, and outcome; and comments about plans and the shape of the wins being developed.

Much of the basic information required for a full-scale RAM program currently exists in computerized form in most midsize to large companies. These include databases of employees, former employees, retirees, customers, prospects, suppliers, and shareholders. As is often the case, the technical and operational problem is one of integrating and enhancing these databases with the right systems for the specific purpose, which here would be to support a RAM program. Achieving the required integration would be a nontrivial task. In our enterprises, we are now able to build RAM considerations into our systems when they're being specified and developed. Not every company has that advantage. However, we believe that efforts to systematize RAM to some extent, either with *de novo* systems or by adapting existing internal systems or with products such as Goldmine, to the needs of a RAM effort will more than repay themselves.

A RAM ROADMAP

The following flowchart can serve as a useful roadmap for implementing a RAM strategy. It depicts just one way of organizing the elements of a RAM program because every RAM strategy has unique features. The elements and activities could be broken down further, and they should be made more specific for any company embarking on a RAM effort.

However they are organized, the high-level steps—evaluate relationships in light of goals, success factors, and risks; have an owner for each relationship; define wins for all parties; and move the relationship into the win-win zone—and the operational tasks and activities—research, cultivation, contact, connection, bonding, building trust, defining and delivering wins, conducting maintenance and repair—will invariably produce the desired results if they are implemented in a logical and consistent manner.

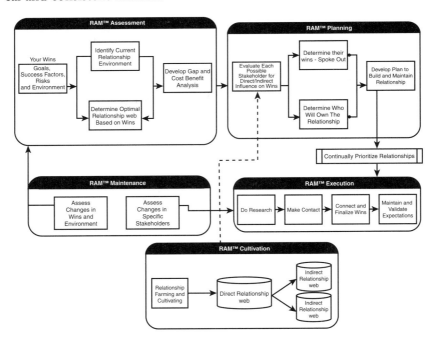

A RAM roadmap.

- RAM requires changes in thinking and behavior in relationships, and people and organizations resist change. Therefore, the RAM Sell justifies the effort and generates momentum.

- Gap analysis gauges the difference between the current Relationship Web and the ideal one. Cost-benefit analysis compares RAM to other, more traditional methods of accomplishing tasks. For the tasks that RAM is suited to, it will generally be the most cost-effective method available.

- A RAM assessment, done to set up a program or to monitor an ongoing one, reveals the condition of the relationship, the balance of wins, and the value and potential value.

- Relationships change, and losing one is a setback. RAM insurance in its various forms aims to prevent such losses.

- RAM insurance includes creating multiple links, using written contracts, making stakeholders part of the business, and conducting solid maintenance.

- Relationship assets must be maintained on a schedule, just like vehicles and productive equipment.

- Every RAM plan is unique to the company undertaking it because every company has its own set of goals, success factors, and risks, and its own Relationship Web.

MAXIMIZE THE LONG-TERM VALUE OF RELATIONSHIPS

When I grew up in Brooklyn, my father put a weight bench in our basement. We would go down there at night and lift together. Because my father and I were reaching for the stars. We were trying to get me bigger. So I could one day play for Notre Dame. That's why it felt so great in our locker room that night at the Sugar Bowl. My father was in there with us. My grandfather was there. … We wanted to hold that moment as long as we could.

—*Frank Pomarico, quoted in* Talking Irish: The Oral History of Notre Dame Football, *by Steve Delsohn*

Long-term goals and long-term relationships are the stuff of true success. The long view adopted by Notre Dame's Frank Pomarico and his dad might not be the preferred view in American business, but it is that perspective that most surely brings people to their goals and leads to the best relationships. Holding the long view takes discipline, and it takes a willingness to invest for the long term.

The latest evidence of the dangers of short-term thinking lay in the wreckage of the turn-of-the-millennium dot-com IPO craze. Please know that we believe in the premise and the promise of the Internet as deeply as anyone, but investors chasing short-term gains drove stock prices to unjustifiable heights, misallocated millions of dollars of capital, and misdirected thousands of entrepreneurs and high-tech professionals. At the time, however, investors who focused on the long term and on sound fundamentals were thought of as missing out. Why weren't these "value investors" doubling their money every year? Why were they so committed to companies with "real assets"?

RAM also focuses on the long term and on sound fundamentals. If relationships are indeed assets, then they will, like other assets, either grow or depreciate over time. Passively managed, some will grow and some will depreciate. RAM is a system for actively managing relationship assets so that they grow in value.

In this principle, we examine the value of relationships more deeply and explore ways of prioritizing them to properly gauge the investment they require. But first, let's examine a perfect example of short-term management.

HOW TO KILL A COMPANY

The story of "Chainsaw" Al Dunlap charts an approach that stands at the exact opposite pole from RAM. After all, it is Al Dunlap who once said, "Stakeholders are total rubbish." (The quote is from *Chainsaw: The Notorious Career of Al Dunlap in the Era of Profit-at-Any-Price,* by John A. Byrne, the definitive book on the subject.)

In all fairness, Al Dunlap could not have operated as he did without the encouragement of Wall Street, which richly rewarded greenmail, hostile takeovers, and leveraged buyouts coupled with asset sell-offs in the 1980s, and the plant closings, lay-offs, and downsizing of the 1980s and 1990s. Most observers of the business scene agreed there was fat to be trimmed from many companies. Yet the phenomenon of "corporate anorexia," the result of cutting vital assets, had already been identified by the early 1990s.

Through downsizing, Dunlap did deliver short-term gains. During his 18 months as CEO of Scott Paper, for example, the company's stock price rose 225 percent, increasing market value by $6.3 billion. John Byrne states that "the self-styled turnaround artist fired 11,000 employees, cut all corporate philanthropy, slashed expenditures on plant improvements and research, and then sold the company to a major rival. Wall Street cheered as Scott became the sixth consecutive company that was sold or dismembered by Dunlap since 1983."

"Chainsaw" Al built his career on massive lay-offs and draconian cost-cutting, and Wall Street loved him for it. In mid-1996, when he came to Sunbeam, the 100-year-old manufacturer of toasters, mixers, and other kitchen appliances, the stock, which had been selling at $12.50, shot up 49 percent—in one day.

Eighteen months later, 16 of Sunbeam's 26 factories, 5 of its 6 headquarters, and half of its 12,000 employees were gone. Initially, the company nearly disintegrated. Byrne states, "Departments and functions lacked the people to get a normal day's work done. Plants needed to produce goods for retailers were being shut down." He adds that Wal-Mart, Sunbeam's largest customer, threatened to drop the company as a vendor after losing $9 million in sales on undelivered irons. Computers were down for months. Customers had to be invoiced manually. Technicians making $35,000 a year were laid off and rehired as independent contractors at three or more times their former salaries.

In this environment, Dunlap set the goal of doubling revenues to $2 billion by 1999 and increasing the net margin from 2.5 to 20 percent. New products were supposed to generate $600 million in revenues by that year. Before long, however, managers were resorting to questionable accounting techniques to make their numbers, which was Dunlap's constant (and loud and profane) demand. The most controversial accounting technique was "bill-and-hold," in which retailers agreed to purchase goods that wouldn't be delivered and paid for for several months. This was most famously used with Sunbeam gas grills, which accounted for one third of total revenue.

These problems were brewing throughout 1997, yet in January 1998, Sunbeam's stock hovered around $39 a share. Dunlap remained the darling of Wall Street because he bragged that he cared first and last for a company's shareholders—the only constituency that he genuinely saw as important—and cultivated a "Rambo-in-pinstripes" image.

On June 13, 1998, Dunlap was fired. By July, the SEC had begun investigating the company, a major accounting firm had withdrawn its unqualified opinion of the most recent audit, and Sunbeam was in default on the covenants of its bank loan agreements. The company collapsed as revenues and profits from 1997 up through Dunlap's departure were restated. For 1998, the company lost almost $900 million. In mid-1999, Sunbeam still had not made a profit, and its stock traded in the $5 to $7 range.

The scary thing about Al Dunlap's reign over Sunbeam is that it is only one, admittedly extreme, example of the short-term view that's so prevalent in American business. This view persistently surfaces in new forms: buyouts, break-ups, and asset sell-offs in the 1980s; mass lay-offs and downsizing in the late 1980s and early 1990s; and dot-com madness in the mid- to late 1990s. Scarier still is the fact that it is almost always rewarded by the investment community—in the short term, that is.

When we first started getting RAM down on paper, we ran right up against Al Dunlap's philosophy, which at the time still seemed to be working. Virtually every decision he made with respect to every stakeholder was focused on the short term and skewed toward Wall Street's demands—the antithesis of RAM. Seeing this, we asked ourselves, how could this CEO be so successful while refuting everything that RAM stands for? We forged ahead, but we seriously wondered how we would reconcile our ideas with Dunlap's apparent success. Then Sunbeam imploded and our problem evaporated, along with any misgivings we might have entertained about the value of RAM.

IS RAM COUNTER TO U.S. CULTURE?

Investment houses earn money on activity, such as trades and new issues. Buy-and-hold investors and "patient capital" generate relatively little activity. Thus, to maximize (short-term) profits, Wall Street must stir up activity. Combine that fact with corporate management's goal of maximizing shareholder value—the original phrase "*long-term* shareholder value" is seldom heard—and then mix well with our celebrity- and news-driven business media, and you have a recipe for short-term investing and management. (The January 12, 1998, issue of *Fortune* noted that Al Dunlap "checks Sunbeam's stock price at least eight times daily.")

RAM reorients management toward long-term relationships rather than short-term profits. A short-term perspective is a flawed strategy for creating long-term value. Short-term thinking skews management's decisions toward activities that undermine long-term value. However, RAM and its long-term view run counter not only to the prevailing business ethos but also to certain aspects of the very culture of the United States. Americans are transient, almost nomadic. This land of new ideas, fresh starts, and fast friends could be the easiest place in the world for a person to move on and leave the past behind. People change employers, positions, careers, residences, and marital status with tremendous ease relative to other, typically older, cultures.

The United States styles itself as a throwaway society. Disposable razors, lighters, and cameras dominate their respective product categories. Microwave ovens, televisions, and radios are routinely discarded rather than repaired. Movies, TV shows, and new products have mere weeks to find a market before they're yanked away and replaced. The media goes through "celebrities" so quickly that they're called the Flavor of the Month. These phenomena reflect and reinforce a certain national mind-set: a short attention span, a need for novelty, and a desire for stimulation. Whether we like it or not, these are characteristics of our culture.

The bright side of all this includes optimism about the future, a capacity for self-invention, a sense of adventure, and, in business, an entrepreneurial spirit unmatched in any other culture. Compared with other cultures, we're also more readily able to build relationships across ethnic groups and economic classes. However, the darker side of our culture generates change for the sake of change, undermines tradition, and provides few signposts for navigating a path through life. There's also a tendency to undervalue relationships and, commonly, a lack of desire to work at them.

In this environment, RAM can be a tough sell. Yet it is this very environment that can make RAM a driver of success. If nothing else, building long-term relationships with *all* stakeholders will distinguish a company from most others. Also, at the level of the individual, most Americans long for deeper, longer-term relationships. (Co-workers might find it strange to be invited to your home for dinner, but once there they enjoy themselves and take pleasure in creating a closer relationship.) Nonetheless, managing relationships for the long term demands an understanding of their long-term value, a willingness to invest in them, and the ability to prioritize them and maintain them over time.

A SLOW WAY TO GET RICH QUICK

Up to now, much of our discussion has focused on early-in-the-relationship activities—how to cast a RAM strategy in the context of goals, success factors, and risks; how to identify, research, cultivate, contact, and connect with stakeholders; and how to define and develop mutual wins. With this principle, we shift to a time horizon extending years or decades into the future and over the life of the organization.

UNDERSTANDING THE LONG-TERM VALUE OF RELATIONSHIPS

Only recently have companies formally considered the long-term value of relationships—and then only for customers and employees. For instance, the lifetime value of a customer—the profit generated by a customer over the entire relationship—is a relatively recent notion that has not been universally adopted. Similarly, the cost of acquiring a customer versus retaining one—a ratio that can hit 5:1 to 7:1 or more—has been quantified in few companies. The same holds true for the cost of recruiting and training a new employee versus keeping a current one. Management consultant Dr. Gerald Kraines states that it takes 18 months for a professional who's new to a company to become fully productive. Such factors would have to be considered in accounting for the true cost of replacing an employee.

For other stakeholders, the concept of value becomes harder to express in dollars. What is the value of a good relationship with your congressman? On any random day, few senior managers would give it a thought. But when something happens—for example, a consumer group lobbies for legislation that could affect your business—that relationship with your congressman could quickly become very valuable (provided that there *is* a relationship). A similar value-of-trouble-avoided or value-of-help-when-needed calculus underlies relationships with the media, the community, and competitors and complementors. Recall the attorney who said, "You have to make friends *before* you need them."

Switching costs should be factored into the value of a relationship. As noted in Principle #10, "Get Rolling and Maintain Momentum," a customer switching to another supplier incurs costs. Companies in financial services, information systems, and telecommunications acutely understand that these costs work to keep customers in the relationship.

In other words, the value—to a customer—of continuing the relationship includes the switching costs he avoids. Similarly, the concept of switching costs can be applied to other relationships. If you alienate a lender, you incur the expense and trouble of finding a new one the next time you want a loan. If you lose your media contacts through neglect, you must develop new ones. In a sense, recruiting and training expenses are the "switching costs" of employee turnover.

Ultimately, however, the long-term value of a relationship comes in the form of larger and better wins. Plus, as the relationship progresses, these wins are actually realized at a lower cost. Some companies have found that their most loyal customers not only provide all the profit but also cover losses incurred in dealing with less loyal customers. As is the case for most companies, long-term relationships paid off for SCG. Dollar for dollar, longer-term employees were more productive and required less direction. The minimal sales costs incurred on long-term customers automatically made them more profitable.

The value of other stakeholder relationships increases over time as well. Long-term suppliers know your company and how it operates, making them easier to do business with. The same holds true, only more so, for your bank. Long-standing strategic partners benefit from knowledge of one another's operations, while long-term relationships with government agencies enable you to more easily meet their requirements.

Another mechanism boosts the value of long-term relationships with stakeholders. As we'll discuss shortly, establishing a relationship requires an investment of time, energy, and some expense. That investment in bringing on a customer or employee, in winning the confidence of a banker or investor, and in finding a good supplier or strategic partner is a sunk cost. The longer the relationship exists, the greater the return on that investment.

So, the value of a relationship increases as the parties come to know one another better, work more smoothly together, and, most importantly, get better at developing mutual wins. And the investment in the relationship produces a larger return the longer the relationship lasts and produces wins.

RETURN ON RELATIONSHIPS

The terms "relationship capital" and "return on relationships" have recently entered the business lexicon. They are useful, though vaguely defined, concepts. They're not yet highly quantifiable. However, there are subjective but practical ways to measure relationship capital and your return on relationships.

You know you have relationship capital, and that it is producing a return, when the following are true:

1. You are achieving goals, enhancing success factors, and mitigating risks with the help of a range of stakeholders.

2. Stakeholders bring you interesting deals and solid opportunities.

3. Stakeholders bring other potential stakeholders into your Relationship Web.

4. Potential stakeholders from various sources come to you by word of mouth.

5. People call you for information, advice, and favors (they have relationship capital with you, too, which is the way it should be).

6. Your business achieves well-managed growth in a balanced manner, with customers, employees, suppliers, investors, charities, and other constituents sharing in that growth to the appropriate extent.

7. Your stakeholders demonstrate loyalty by remaining stakeholders over the long term.

8. You know who to call to help you with the problems that commonly (or uncommonly) arise in your business.

9. Your phone calls are returned, you receive invitations to off-the-job events, and you find yourself making friends among your stakeholders.

10. People congratulate you on your achievements—and mean it.

Try using these 10 points as a checklist for gauging the return on specific relationships or on stakeholder groups, preferably with a colleague who also knows the stakeholders. Each point can be rated from 1 to 10 or from poor to excellent. Take a long-term view when measuring return on relationships—wins from long ago or potential wins far in the future count in this analysis.

FROM THE RAM PLAYBOOK

We believe that in the future, the value of a company's relationships will be routinely considered in due diligence and valuations of them will be conducted by potential acquirers, strategic partners, and investors. Such valuations now occur for some relationships, at least implicitly. For instance, a company will often select an acquisition or strategic partner on the basis of its relationships with certain customers, distributors, or international entities.

Productive relationships have as much value as patents, intellectual property, brand equity, and other elements of goodwill (the amount an acquirer pays beyond the value of the tangible assets of the business). Why shouldn't relationship assets count?

Early on at SCG and well before we began to codify RAM, we explicitly considered an entity's relationships when we pursued it. In searching for software vendors to leverage off in our sales process, we targeted those who were already calling on the companies we wanted as clients. At Entente, we considered potential investment partners as much for their relationships as for their capital (more so, in fact).

Today, we use a more formal approach, which closely parallels the RAM assessment presented in Principle 10. Key questions that we pose to managers of potential stakeholder entities include: Who are the company's stakeholders? Which stakeholders do they consider most important?

How long have the key stakeholders been on board? What is the condition of the company's relationships? What is the composition and balance of their Relationship Web? We also ask ourselves: Are there gaps in their web? Can we fill those gaps? What value do we place on their relationships?

As noted, we also carefully check references. All this is by way of learning whether a company's management really sees relationships as assets and treats them as such.

INVESTING IN RELATIONSHIPS

If relationships are assets with long-term value, then it makes business sense to invest resources to develop and maintain them. That insight can dispel any lingering short-term views or Chainsaw Al–type ideas you might still be harboring. When you believe and perceive that relationships are valuable, long-term assets, you become willing to invest in them.

The investment, as noted in Principle #10, is time, creativity, and energy, as well as money. We start from the premise that most relationship owners and other employees who deal with stakeholders are already contacting them. The investment—in existing relationships—comes when relationship owners are asked to boost their contact efforts, keep more complete records, and work harder to create win-win scenarios. That represents a relatively small incremental investment because the relationships are already "in the house." For most companies under-taking RAM, the larger investment will be in developing a larger-scale, more ambitious cultivation or "farming" effort. Cultivation—identifying, researching, contacting, and regularly touching potential stakeholders—forms the foundation of an ongoing RAM effort.

Most people fail to cultivate a large number of potential stakeholders for one simple reason: They see no immediate value and no near-term win for themselves. Thus, they say "Why bother?" They don't realize that the investment in cultivation pays off down the road when you and the other party see the opportunity to create a mutual win.

For high-potential relationships, we suggest that you invest even more. Go beyond cultivation and regular touches, and provide a proactive win. If you can help a potential stakeholder by giving him a tip, a name, or some help, or by enabling him to capitalize on an opportunity—and do so with a reasonable investment of time, money, and effort—then you've created trust. You have also started to accrue relationship capital. You've invested in an asset.

Is providing a proactive win just working things so that someone "owes you one"? No, by virtue of your commitment to create a win-win relationship, or no relationship at all. Demanding a win from someone, or expecting an outsized or one-sided win because you helped them out, hardly conforms to the spirit of RAM. The proactive win creates trust. If you make demands or "call in markers," you diminish that trust. RAM says, start building a relationship on that trust. If you provide a proactive win and then fail to create a bond and get to know the person, you've missed an opportunity.

Investments in relationships yield returns, but the "investment horizon" is typically the long term. Some relationships get off to a fast start. The right players find the right opportunity, and—bang! They're creating big wins from day one. It's great when it happens, and, with a large, well-cultivated Relationship Web, it will happen. But rather than think of early stage relationships as win-win, you might think of them as win-someday/win relationships.

Investing in RAM can and should be fun. You can keep hundreds and even thousands of contacts alive by touching them every few months. Developing ways of doing that, conducting your research, getting to know stakeholders, and always working toward mutual wins presents one of the most worthwhile challenges in business. It's a challenge that we're all better off accepting.

RAM PRIORITIZATION

Because RAM requires an investment, you must invest the available RAM resources, so to speak, where they will produce the greatest return.

We have emphasized that every stakeholder is important, but the fact is that some—by virtue of several factors, which we'll examine here—are more important than others. Therefore, relationships must be prioritized, and their priority must be used to allocate resources to developing and maintaining them.

The key determinant of priority is the value of the relationship. That's why it's important to know the value of your relationships to your company and to the stakeholder, even if it's an approximate concept. When you consider the value to both parties, you focus on the total value to be created and the total of the wins to be shared—and RAM exists to make that pie bigger. Also, note that value and priority are two different things, and their correlation is high but not perfect. Value will usually be the strongest factor in setting priority, yet it is still just one factor.

Before we examine factors to use in prioritizing relationships, three caveats are in order. First, priority, by its nature, is a relative concept. The only reason to prioritize anything is that there are more than one of them. So, all relationships are important, but they often have different priority—that is, different relative importance—at a given time. Generally, employee and customer relationships are top priorities and command more resources than most other groups, but other stakeholders have their priorities, too.

Second, priorities can shift rapidly. This happened recently in the technology industry, where, before the year 2000 tech-stock shakeout, companies gave employees priority. In the rush to land talent, they dangled signing bonuses, stock options, onsite massages, and other perks in front of job candidates. They assigned lower priority to customers, who were flocking to the Web anyway, and to investors, who were throwing money at entrepreneurs. Since the shakeout, the priority has shifted away from employees (many of whom are no longer employed) and toward customers, who now demand value from the Web, and investors, who have become extremely selective. And the priorities will undoubtedly shift again.

Third, as is the case for most RAM analyses, prioritizing relationships—whether quarterly (highly recommended) or ad hoc (often necessary)—should be done by at least two people familiar with the relationship. The CRO and, in some cases, another senior manager, along with the relationship owner and perhaps another contact person, would be likely participants in the process.

With this background in mind, you'll find the following criteria, which can be weighted and assigned scores, useful in prioritizing relationships:

Urgent problems: An urgent problem affecting a stakeholder or stakeholder group can move that relationship to top priority. At those times, remember that other stakeholders still retain some priority. In fact, a serious enough problem in a valuable relationship—such as one that could result in the loss of a large customer, key employees, or a major investor—will almost always affect other stakeholders. Their interests must be safeguarded as well.

For example, at the congressional hearing that Sen. Hollings described as a catfight, Ford and Firestone lost sight of all other stakeholder relationships—including their relationship with one another—in their efforts to escape blame before the government and the public. The relationship with the congressional committee was clearly a high priority, but other relationships still counted.

Historical value: In general, the longer a stakeholder relationship exists, the more valuable it becomes. However, that does not automatically translate to high priority. If anything, such a relationship might require few resources relative to its value. We're not implying that long-standing stakeholders can be taken for granted, but there's often a comfort level and well-established patterns of contact and mutual wins that demand fewer RAM resources to maintain.

If a long-standing relationship becomes dormant and fresh thinking could multiply the wins, then a RAM revival could be in order. That revival would raise the relationship's priority.

Potential value: Both long-standing and new relationships should be judged on their perceived future value to both parties. If you've just taken on a new supplier or distributor, the relationship will require an up-front investment to reach its full potential. Anticipating the wins down the road—in every relationship—will help you gauge the amount of resources to invest in building and maintaining the relationship.

Potential value is important in another way. Some relationships take years, literally, to deliver all their potential wins, and that must be understood. For example, in the television industry, the networks are regularly assailed for not sticking long enough with a high-quality show, usually defined as one garnering critical praise and a small but loyal base of viewers. Many television shows that became huge hits, including *Seinfeld,* didn't catch on with the broader public until their second or third season.

Don't throw good money after bad, but don't invest in developing a relationship only to abandon it prematurely.

Potential for conflict: Factors ranging from the mix of personalities to overlapping business interests can heighten the potential for conflict. That, in turn, heightens the priority of a relationship.

The way that many companies handle their R&D or new product development units is illustrative. Companies that place high priority on new products often set up those operations separately from headquarters and the operating units. Bell Labs was a separate entity even before the breakup of AT&T. IBM, based in New York and North Carolina, set up a separate unit in Florida to develop its PC. Why? Because the potential for conflict between creative engineers and operating personnel is high. R&D produces numerous failures and distant payoffs. Operating units produce cash in the present and deal with day-to-day issues. Misunderstanding and resentment between the two groups can run high. When product development has priority, giving R&D people elbow room allows them, as well as the operating people, to work without interference.

Third-party issues: When a relationship with a stakeholder can affect a third party, particularly one you both deal with, crank up the priority. How much depends on the third party and the potential effect on them. If that third party could benefit greatly or be seriously hurt by the status of or the actions within a relationship, raise its priority. Also think in terms of the Relationship Web: Relationships are interrelated, and the web metaphor can help you "connect the dots."

As the cases of Microsoft and its competitors and of Ford (a customer) and Firestone (a supplier) demonstrate, government agencies represent a potential third party that must be considered. In addition, a hidden third party—a powerful stakeholder of your stakeholder who is unknown to you—can create problems. Get as much information about your stakeholders' stakeholders as you reasonably can, and then give them every reasonable consideration.

Natural affinity and personal connections: If the owner and the stakeholder "click" or have a strong personal bond, the priority can move either up or down. Personal affinity can turbocharge a business relationship, making it smoother and multiplying the wins. That might mean that the entity can assign it a lower priority for more formal RAM efforts.

Yet you can never expect a personal relationship between an employee and a stakeholder to carry the day. In fact, a strong personal bond could signal the need to establish multiple links to that stakeholder, thus providing some RAM insurance.

The team that's prioritizing the relationship can rate each one on a scale of one to five on each of these factors, as we do. The scores can then be reconciled through discussion. That discussion and the resulting final revised scores will provide a good idea of RAM priorities and a basis for allocating resources to building and maintaining relationships.

CREATE A FLEXIBLE ROSTER

Stakeholder relationships must be prioritized at every level of the organization, from the executive committee to the individual relationship owners, at both regular intervals and in response to changes. How stakeholders are prioritized and how their priority drives the allocation of RAM resources depends on the company. The result of the process, however, should be an integrated—rather than conflicting—set of priorities that people can use as a guide.

That guide must be flexible. Stakeholders' priority will inevitably shift with economic events, business conditions, and changes on the stakeholders' side. For instance, in a tight job market, relationships with sources of talented candidates and with employees themselves rise in priority. When costs need to be cut, strategic allies and independent contractors rise in priority. Customers are always a priority, yet in a seller's market, marketing programs might decrease in priority relative to efforts to secure capital for expansion. Those efforts would increase the priority of lenders and investors.

Prioritizing relationships enables you clearly see two things. First, you'll see that no single stakeholder group—investors, employees, or even customers—can *always* have top priority. With this insight, you can respond more quickly to change. Second, you'll improve your process of allocating resources. Most budgeting processes allocate funds in terms of facilities, equipment, head counts, and standard efforts, such as new product development and marketing programs. Bringing the company's relationships into the budgeting process reminds managers that there are people—and, thus, relationship assets—affected by every decision, for better or worse.

STAYING STEADFAST IN A CHANGING WORLD

Maintaining relationships for years or decades takes special effort, and it's well worth it.

Consider what the effect would be on your business, your career, and your life if you had kept in touch on some level with even 20 percent of the people that you've gone to school with, worked with, or met in a business context. What if you had used even the most basic RAM techniques—a bit of research and a regular schedule of touches, coupled with some thought about mutual wins—to cultivate relationships with those people?

Over the years, that kind of effort has placed each of us in regular contact with 2,500 to 3,000 people in some way and at some interval. In total, these folks have helped us, and we've helped them, in almost every conceivable business situation, including sales prospecting, closing deals, searching for talent, conducting job searches, raising funds, gaining publicity, generating word-of-mouth, and exchanging advice and information on people, places, and purchases. They've nominated us for the occasional award and supported our businesses directly, as in their choice of restaurant when they dine out. Even with infrequent contact and in peripheral (or what we think of as potential) relationships, we've enriched each other's lives, if only by passing on a joke or a tip.

Now consider what the impact would be if you had made a concerted effort to take RAM to the next level—to develop clear mutual wins and a bond of trust with some percentage of that 20 percent of the people you've known.

Staggering thought, isn't it?

Picture yourself driving down a highway. It's a beautiful day. You've got the window rolled down. And as you cruise on down the road, you are throwing $20 bills out that window. That is exactly what you are doing when you let relationships slip through your hands.

If the only thing you take away from this book is a deep belief that every relationship is potentially valuable, then our writing it and your reading it has been worthwhile. When people come into your life and you let them leave without a trace, when you make no effort to establish contact or a common bond, and when you give no thought to how you can help one another succeed, it is exactly as if you are throwing your money out the window.

The people whom you need and who need you in order to succeed are all around you. You'll meet dozens of them, perhaps hundreds, in the months ahead. When you do, find out who they are and what they want. Follow up with them. Tell them it was good to meet them and that you hope you can get together on something in the future. Think win-win and long term—and then act on that thinking. Then hold on tight as your career and your business take off and achieve speeds and heights that you never thought were possible.

FROM THE RAM PLAYBOOK

Many University of Miami Sigma Chis of the early 1980s have maintained friendships and business relationships for almost 20 years. Pregame tailgate parties during the Miami Hurricanes football season are the vehicle for staying in touch. We arrive at the stadium early and spend time with one another and our families for a few games per season.

In this way, we maintain tradition, contact, and personal and business bonds, and we get to see one another gain weight, lose hair, and interact with loved ones. This is the only time in the year that most of us see one another. But we continue to do business with a number of the guys we met all those years ago and stayed in touch with over the tailgate.

- Taking a long-term view of business relationships might run counter to what Wall Street rewards (in the short term) and to what U.S. culture reinforces, yet long-term value represents the most accurate gauge of success.

- Dollar valuations can be calculated for some relationships, notably those with customers and employees, while for other stakeholders they will be more approximate. Nevertheless, if applied consistently, any reasonable means of valuation will give you an idea of the relative value of your relationships.

- Investing in relationships means putting resources into cultivating and maintaining relationships. Although near-term payoffs do occur, it's best to adopt a long-term investment horizon.

- Key considerations in prioritizing relationships include urgent problems, historical and potential value, potential for conflict, third-party issues, and personal connections.

- A stakeholder's priority for allocation of RAM resources can change. Therefore, the priorities of the company and the relationship owners must be flexible.

- Relationships must be prioritized periodically as well as constantly, in response to changing conditions.

- Each of us has myriad opportunities to form win-win relationships. To let those opportunities slip through our hands is literally to throw money out the window.

PRINCIPLE #12:

KEEP THE WINS COMING, STAKEHOLDER BY STAKEHOLDER

The real fun of the game will always lie in good hard batting, hard throwing and hard running. … Then, whether you win the game or lose it, you will savor the deep satisfaction of having done your very best, of having turned on your strength and speed to the very limit of your supply. "Well," you can tell yourself whatever the outcome, "I gave it all I've got and it was a great ball game."

—*From* Hit Hard! Throw Hard! The Secrets of Power Baseball, *by Robert Smith*

At bottom, RAM is about giving every relationship with every stakeholder your very best. Doing so will create more mutual wins and greater success, and will also bring you greater professional and personal satisfaction. By way of further assisting you, we provide here our thoughts on doing business with specific stakeholder groups. This compilation does not include every stakeholder group a company could have, nor does it cover every aspect of doing business with them. That would be impossible. Yet while these notes on stakeholders are representative rather than all-inclusive, they should highlight the potential value that's waiting to be mined in all relationships.

While reading this chapter, you might find it useful to refer to the appendix, "Target Wins for Company-Stakeholder Relationships," which provides sample target wins for companies and stakeholder groups.

NOTES ON SPECIFIC STAKEHOLDERS

We believe that the truly unique feature of RAM is its focus on managing *all* stakeholder relationships for maximum long-term value. This feature is also a major source of its power. However, *all* stakeholders covers a lot of ground, so these notes provide a starting point for understanding selected stakeholders, including several that few companies devote many resources to cultivating.

EMPLOYEES: THE FOUNDATION OF RAM

Management's relationship with employees forms the core of the entire relationship asset portfolio. Management, by definition, is the art and science of getting things done through others. Even in a small company, the managers cannot conduct every interaction with every stakeholder. Therefore, employees must practice RAM with everyone they touch. They will do that only if managers view—and treat—their relationships with employees as valuable assets. RAM cannot work on a "do-as-we-say, not-as-we-do" basis.

Management consultant Peter Drucker has stated, "All organizations now routinely say, 'People are our greatest asset.' Yet few practice what they preach, let alone truly believe it." If people are an asset, management will invest in them. The practices used by the outfits in *Fortune*'s annual list of the "100 Best Companies to Work For" all represent an investment in, as well as wins for, employees. Employees clearly appreciate health insurance, onsite daycare and fitness centers, profit sharing, stock options, tuition reimbursement, retirement benefits, employee discounts, flexible hours, personal time, first-class cafeterias, company cars, and corporate concierges. However, each management team must decide—with input from employees, when possible—which benefits will represent the most desired wins.

FROM THE RAM PLAYBOOK

Having a voice in decisions that affect them is an important win for most employees. At SCG, we involved employees in these decisions whenever possible. We quickly learned that it created a better result with less effort. For instance, as our growth ramped up, we saw that our benefits plan was inadequate. Rather than develop a plan unilaterally, we turned it over to the employees. We said, "Try to find something that makes sense for us as employers and for you, too."

They developed a plan that gave them better benefits at a lower cost than we anticipated. And they had ownership of it. This might be impossible in a large company, but in our firm we found it very effective.

We used this approach with other issues, too. Being men, we weren't well suited to develop a maternity leave policy. So, we asked the women in the company to formulate one. They defined a great plan that related paid maternity leave to the length of service with the company. Also, after a few weeks, a new mother could do certain things from home for compensation while she was on leave. In addition, a committee of five employees helped us develop our noncompete contract.

These guidelines can help managers build rich relationships with their employees:

- Plan carefully and then give people clear expectations and the authority, resources, and time to meet those expectations.

- Provide fair compensation, benefits, and participation in long-term growth in keeping with marketplace realities, and compensate management reasonably rather than excessively.

- Recognize that employees have lives and needs outside the company, and provide time and a culture that reflects that reality.

- Ask employees for input, use it whenever possible, and empower them to make decisions (particularly those that affect customers).

- Ensure that immediate supervisors and managers are well-trained, committed to RAM, and suited to their jobs.

- Supply frequent feedback, both positive (in public) and negative (in private), on an ad hoc and scheduled basis.

CUSTOMERS: WITHOUT THEM THERE IS NOTHING

With strong employee relationships in place, customer satisfaction and loyalty will increase *if* the owners of customer relationships—and all others who touch customers—identify the customer's wins and deliver them. A company that consistently performs those two tasks will build long-term customer relationships.

Is it worth it? Ample evidence says that satisfied customers are loyal and profitable, and that long-term relationships are indeed valuable. A Xerox analysis revealed that customers who rated themselves "very satisfied" were six times more likely to purchase Xerox equipment again than "satisfied" customers. At Taco Bell, stores in the top quartile in customer satisfaction ratings outperform the rest of the stores on all other ratings. The company linked managers' compensation to customer satisfaction ratings, and satisfaction *and* profits increased. *Harvard Business Review* noted that some companies found that their most loyal customers—the top 20 percent—not only provided all the profits but also covered the losses incurred in doing business with less loyal customers.

Satisfied customers will be your best source of referrals to new customers. Be sure to ask for those referrals and to thank the customer somehow, preferably with a tangible win, such as a discount or premium. Consider the expense an investment in the new customer relationship. Also consider sales prospects to be active members of your Relationship Web. They might not need your product or service today, but they could next week or next year. Meanwhile, they might send you referrals (don't forget to ask) to give you a win and build goodwill for the day when they do need you.

Also, know who your true customers are, and maintain a direct relationship with them whenever possible. For instance, a restaurant equipment manufacturer operated through independent distributors and thought of these distributors, who sold and serviced the equipment, as its customers. The manufacturer had a small sales force for national accounts, but it also gave those accounts to the distributors to service. In effect, the manufacturer gave ownership of the real customer relationship—the one with the restaurants—to independent distributors. Bad idea.

The distributors were definitely independent. When the manufacturer wanted to research restaurants about the equipment, the distributors were slow to share "their" customer information. They refused to share any service data. A damaging stand-off developed and left the manufacturer with little recourse but to reconfigure its sales and service system.

The better a company knows all its "customers"—decision-makers, end users, influencers, technical staff, service providers, and middlemen—and builds win-win relationships with them, the more stable the platform for current sales and future growth.

In applying RAM strategy to customers, keep these things in mind:

- Foster a genuine sense of ownership for customer relationships throughout the company.
- Avoid adversarial customers and those who negotiate only on the basis of price. The former will make you miserable, and the latter will soon be gone—and neither will be very profitable.
- Collect only the customer information that you can use, and always respect customers' privacy.
- Realize that customer relationship management (CRM) software systems will capture information and perhaps enable you to "sell harder," but the real power comes from combining the information with a RAM strategy.
- Balance wins for customers against those of employees, shareholders, and other stakeholders. Maintaining low prices by underpaying your employees, pounding your suppliers, or starving your shareholders won't work in the long run.

SUPPLIERS: PARTNERS IN SUCCESS

Many companies take an adversarial approach toward suppliers. In a free-market economy, buyers have choices. That positions them to say no, which gives them more power in the situation. Traditionally, purchasing managers have used their buying power to hammer down prices and push for other concessions by playing suppliers off one another. We're not saying that negotiating a low price is bad, but it shouldn't be the sole focus. There's typically more value to be had by using RAM with suppliers, in addition to negotiating the best price.

An adversarial, totally price-driven approach is risky and at times flawed from both the economic and the RAM standpoints. From the economic standpoint, it assumes that the lowest price yields the greatest value in a supplier relationship. From the RAM standpoint, it assumes that supplier relationships are not worth cultivating, that suppliers are interchangeable. We believe the greatest value comes from bringing suppliers into your processes and encouraging them to add greater value wherever they can. This shifts the relationship from adversarial to cooperative, and encourages each party to share its vision, information, and skills. Generally, such a relationship yields the best overall value, including price and service, from suppliers.

Here's how Kevin Harron, president of Tedesco, a franchisee of Outback Steakhouses, sees it:

> "In the restaurant business, produce is usually bought on the basis of price. You go around, get quotes, and go with the lowest. But we have one produce supplier and we do $3 million a year with him, and we've been doing business with him for five years. We have a very strong relationship. That way, I know that if a walk-in cooler cuts out some evening, he'll have a refrigerator truck down there to help us. And he knows that he has $3 million of business he can count on every year."

That's RAM at its best, building a relationship with a supplier in a business where the purchase decision is usually driven by price. Tedesco/Outback and its supplier stay in the win-win zone, where they can count on one another.

In managing relationships with suppliers, follow these guidelines:

- Conduct enough research on the supplier's business to understand, or at least discuss, which financial wins are—and are not—possible.
- Share information about your business to a prudent extent, and pass on any leads, marketplace developments, or upcoming changes in your buying patterns.
- Establish multiple contacts between your company and the supplier to improve the service you receive and to ensure that the relationship runs smoothly during personnel changes.

- Forge a common vision with suppliers, and bring them into your product development and production processes (especially if you are a smaller company that hasn't done so—most large companies have).

INVESTORS: CAN THEY BE SATISFIED?

All investors want the same basic win: a good return, given the perceived risk of the investment. However, this basic win leaves wide room for variances. A "good return" and "perceived risk" vary from investor to investor. Also, investors range from frantic day traders to long-term shareholders, from pension funds managing huge portfolios to individuals holding stock in a single company. Finally, RAM applies not just to investors in public companies but also to backers of private firms and to venture capitalists aiming to take the company public some day. It's a mixed bag.

Private companies are well-positioned to develop relationships with their investors. Often the investors know, or come to know, management personally. Yet many private companies fail to tap the full value of those investors, which goes well beyond their financial contributions. With their vested interest in the company's success, these people usually will share their experience and open their networks to management. The guidance and introductions that these typically successful individuals bring to the enterprise is there for the asking, so be sure to ask.

Senior executives of public companies can and should know their largest investors, but with most shareholders, a personal relationship is out of the question. "Dear Shareholder" is as personal as it gets with most investors in large companies. But that doesn't mean that a corporate investor relations function cannot create long-term relationships with shareholders.

It isn't easy, but over time a company can communicate with investors, analysts, and the media in ways that will attract the kind of investors it wants. People invest largely on the basis of the company's story. The story encompasses management's methods and style, market position and growth strategy, investment priorities, and the company's major contracts and strategic alliances. And many investors, aware of transaction costs and the difficulty of finding a good alternative investment, do buy and hold stock. If management has a long-term strategy and consistently delivers what it says it will, it can attract these investors. Aside from that, good relationships with the media and analysts will go a long way toward ensuring good relations with investors.

Despite our belief that Wall Street's short-term focus distorts management's behavior, we also firmly believe that shareholders deserve their wins. But balancing the wins for all stakeholders over the long term should dominate management's thinking. Long-term relationships with investors depend on steady growth with good returns for the level of risk. RAM charts a course toward that goal by helping companies manage all stakeholder relationships well. When a company does that, investors will see—and share in—the results.

Using RAM strategy with investors entails:

- Recognizing the responsibility of maximizing long-term value for the owners/shareholders.

- Implementing an investor relations effort with a specific relationship owner and the resources to work closely and responsively with the media and analytical community.

- Building relationships with the institutional investors that you want buying your stock.

- Understanding socially conscious investors and activist shareholders, considering their positions, and making any warranted changes to policies and practices.

- Recognizing that many investors are also employees, customers, suppliers, educators, and members of the community.

STRATEGIC ALLIES: MARRIAGES MADE IN HEAVEN OR HELL

Globalization, escalating R&D costs, and shorter product life cycles boosted domestic and international alliances involving U.S. companies by more that 25 percent annually in the 1990s. (We use the term "strategic alliance" to include corporate partnerships, joint ventures, licensing arrangements, and other combinations of separate companies' resources.) Done properly, alliances create wins for both parties, most notably access to skills, processes, technologies, and markets—and relationships—that neither company could develop quickly or cheaply enough. Done poorly, however, alliances are less than the sum of their parts.

The first question in considering an alliance is the basic RAM question: Will this arrangement help the company reach a goal, enhance a success factor, or mitigate a risk? If not, avoid it. Too many alliances are based on vague notions of "sharing resources" or "working on something together." Corporate holding companies often thrust their own subsidiaries into these situations by asking them to "create synergy" with one another without clear goals and financial wins for pursuing them.

The partners' capabilities must complement one another. For instance, credit card giant MBNA began doing business with Southern States Banking Association (SSBA) in the early 1980s. The association had been started by Texas banks to handle their credit card transactions. It didn't make financial sense for each bank to have such an operation. Thus, SSBA's computer systems were set up to handle each bank's accounts separately. This complemented MBNA's growth strategy, which was to cultivate relationships with large groups, such as the National Dental Association, and sign up their members for credit cards. SSBA could easily adapt its system for handling various banks' accounts to handle various affinity groups' accounts.

By the late 1980s, SSBA had established an operation in Delaware, MBNA's home state. Eventually, MBNA acquired some SSBA stock, and later the two companies merged. It all began with the two companies, as customer and supplier and then as partners, combining complementary resources: MBNA's marketing and SSBA's transaction processing.

It takes effort and commitment to make an alliance work. Large companies must control a tendency toward arrogance when approached by smaller companies. The "we're-the-big-boys" attitude cuts off communication—and often the relationship. Problems also arise when companies of any size meet to explore possible synergies, have a promising dialog, and then see nothing happen. It's usually because no one owns the relationship and no one is charged with creating value from the alliance. The effort to solve such problems is worth expending because a well-defined, well-managed strategic alliance will require far less work and expense than building or buying the capabilities gained.

To apply RAM strategy to strategic alliances and partnerships, be sure to do the following:

- Take time to get to know one another so that you know it will work in reality as well as "on paper."
- Set the expectations of wins with the precision of a diamond cutter.
- Craft a clear understanding, in writing, of which party owns existing and to-be-developed assets, such as intellectual property and proprietary processes.
- Have time frames both for goals and for the review and renewal of the partnership agreement (if either party sees no continued win, a longer-term contract won't keep that party productively in the partnership).

BANKS AND OTHER LENDERS: NEVER SAY "IT'S ONLY MONEY"

For most of the past century, banking was extremely relationship-oriented. That changed in the 1970s, when the financial options open to businesses (and individuals) exploded, competition heated up, and banks began luring customers away from one another. These trends changed the nature of banking, but it is still possible and beneficial to cultivate relationships with bankers.

We were able to do so at SCG years before we founded a bank ourselves. For instance, given SCG's growth objectives, we needed ready access to money and wanted a good banking relationship because it makes doing business easier in terms of credit references and so on. So, when we were still small, we got to know our account officer and branch manager personally. We chatted when we stopped in, had lunch, and played golf together. We shared our business plan, both early on and as we grew. We invited our account officer and his boss to our office parties. When we hit *Inc.* magazine's list of growth companies, we sent him copies. Those magazines and parties helped the account officer show his manager that he had picked a winner when he brought SCG into the bank.

As a result of our relationship (and SCG's performance), we were granted an unsecured credit line that eventually reached $3 million. Not bad for a service firm with no inventory, leased offices, and minimal equipment. There is and always will be a subjective aspect to extending credit. If the lender actually knows the prospective borrower, he can ask himself: Are these people trustworthy? Can I believe their projections? Are they determined to succeed? Positive answers to these questions address that subjective side of the credit decision. A relationship helps in other ways, too. When we needed auto loans, our account officer facilitated the process, and if snafus arose with payroll checks or the availability of funds, he was happy to straighten things out.

In applying RAM strategy to banks, follow these strategies:

- Pick the right size bank for your needs. If you need sophisticated services, you might have to go large, but otherwise smaller tends to be more personal.
- Get to know your account officers, and they will feel they have a stake in the business beyond their financial interest. Treat them as partners, as you would a supplier.

- Provide clear, realistic financial projections and business plans. Share them with the banker before you need a loan so she can envision your company's future.

- With any creditor, be sure to communicate often and openly if you owe money and are having financial difficulties. Develop a plan for improvement and repayment, and stick with it.

- Bankers like updates on how their business accounts are doing, not only for the information but in acknowledgment of their role in the company. You won't have to work very hard to find reasons to keep in touch with your banker, and it's definitely worth doing.

MEDIA: GETTING THE BUZZ

Media outlets have pressing needs, which they must meet every day, week, or month, depending on their schedules. This is as true in the business-oriented media as in any other segment, and, in the past decade, very few segments have grown as quickly. In this atmosphere, you can readily position yourself to provide wins for the media. Your basic target win, of course, is good publicity—a positive message delivered to the right audience in the right medium. The right audience is the specific stakeholder group you want to reach. The right medium is the publication your audience reads or the program it watches. Therefore, RAM strategy dictates that you first get to know your stakeholders' reading, viewing, and listening habits and then build relationships with people in those media.

For example, at SCG we primarily wanted to reach CIOs and IT managers. So, we sought relationships with editors at publications those stakeholders read. Now that we own a restaurant, everyone who dines out is a potential customer. So, we target local mass-market publications, such as the *Miami Herald*. In addition, Tim Hardaway's involvement gives us a sports angle, so we seek coverage on shows such as the NBA's *Inside Stuff* and on sports segments of the news, which use the restaurant as a setting for interviews and so on.

Depending on your needs, your priority might be to deliver a message to investors, potential employees, customers, or the community. Virtually any group can be reached through specialized publications or the mass media, or both. Yet, as we've pointed out, relationships with major newspapers, general-interest magazines, and business magazines such as *Fortune, Business Week,* and *Forbes* can be tough to establish and maintain. You might well receive a greater return for your efforts by cultivating smaller, more tightly focused publications.

We live in a culture dominated by the media. Yet RAM takes personal relationships as the true medium of human interaction. In that context, editors, journalists, and producers should be treated like everyone else. However, the media also views its biggest win as informing and stimulating the audience, so handle with care.

When applying RAM to the media, follow these tips:

- PR differs from advertising. When you advertise, you get the message you want into print because you pay the publication to run it. With publicity, the editor has the final say.

- Be attuned to the editor's agenda and wins. Even those at publications that never print negative articles don't like to run "puff pieces"—stories that toot a company's horn without delivering value to readers.

- Ask for the editorial calendar of your target publications so you know what special issues and major features are coming up, and then tailor your pitches properly.

- Submit story ideas through a freelance PR person or on-staff publicist, unless you want to learn how to write query letters and articles. Or, hire a public relations firm and work closely with it.

- Maintain contact with journalists, editors, and producers as they move around in this high-turnover business—and get to know their replacements.

- Remember that the media influences all your other stakeholders. Make sure you mine all the value of that influence.

COMPLEMENTORS AND COMPETITORS: FRIENDS AND FOES?

We define complementors as companies that play a role in the same business, without doing business with one another. Although they don't interact directly, their products, services, or operations are somehow linked. Chip manufacturers and software manufacturers are excellent examples. Both sell to computer manufacturers and don't sell to each other (except in small amounts). The fortunes of complementors tend to rise and fall together. Therefore, every company should know its complementors and talk with them. Then, when they face a common threat or joint opportunity, they can join forces faster and with more trust in one another.

FROM THE RAM PLAYBOOK

At Horizon Bank, we watch for ways to create wins for competitors. For instance, the 100 Black Men of Broward County (a nonprofit organization promoting the interests of minority families and businesses in South Florida) introduced us to Wittenauer, the watch manufacturer, which was relocating to Fort Lauderdale. The company wanted a loan that was too large for the bank, given its size. So, we introduced them to another, larger bank that could make the loan.

Often, helping a competitor generates multiple wins, as it did in this case. The larger bank won by painlessly booking a good loan. Wittenauer won by getting its loan with minimal fuss. The 100 Black Men organization won by enhancing its relationship with the company (and Horizon Bank). And Horizon enhanced its relationship with the larger bank, with the company, and with the nonprofit organization.

More broadly, we're cultivating relationships with other banks—our competitors—for three reasons. First, we believe in the industry tradition of banks supporting one another to keep the banking system healthy. Second, we want to work with other banks to develop, purchase, share, and sell loans. Third, as investors, we're aware that mergers and acquisitions are a great way to grow a bank quickly. We'll improve our chances of finding good candidates by doing business with potential partners as we go along.

SCG's relationship with software vendors (as recounted in Principle #1, "See Relationships as Valuable Assets") shows two complementors working and winning together. The vendors sold software that required implementation. We were consultants who implemented software. We helped them win sales by customizing their demos. They helped us win sales by introducing us to their clients. There was no formal alliance, yet the arrangement worked extremely well.

Regarding competitors, most companies take an aggressive posture, yet more are fraternizing across "enemy lines" than ever. For example, Xerox and Hewlett Packard are competitors e in printers and copying machines, but they're partners in other ventures. Such companies have found that they have wins to gain in areas where they don't compete.

In some industries, competitors cooperate for their collective good. For instance, until the mid-1990s, cruise lines spent heavily on marketing to attract vacationers away from one another. Then an industry survey revealed that only 3 percent of the American public had ever taken a cruise vacation. This finding prompted a new line of thought: Instead of fighting over this small market, why not band together to market the joys of cruise vacations in general? They did exactly that and called a truce until follow-up surveys showed that a larger percentage of the public was taking cruise vacations. Then they resumed their fight for share of an expanded market.

The following guidelines can help complementors and competitors work together:

- Communicate with complementors and competitors, particularly through industry and professional associations.

- Try to define areas of competition and of potential cooperation, where you both could achieve larger wins by working together.

- Emulate the cruise industry, if possible. Growing the whole pie by sharing resources might well boost everyone's business.

- Use care in hiring people away from competitors and when your people leave for a competitor. Guard your proprietary products and processes with contracts, patents, copyrights, and trademarks.

- Don't drive your competitors to band together against you (as Microsoft did). And always remember that today's competitor can be tomorrow's strategic ally or merger partner.

UNIVERSITIES: GET SMART

Knowledgee , talent, and intellectual horsepower now represent key success factors in business. This means that most companies can benefit by building relationships with colleges and universities. However, there are few stakeholders that companies ignore more frequently. The loss to each party can be substantial because companies and colleges can provide numerous very practical wins for each other.

Colleges play a strong role in their communities. They attract a constant stream of new residents who patronize local businesses, need employment upon (and before) graduation, and often remain in the area the rest of their lives. Administrators and faculty play leadership roles in their cities, and they, too, support local businesses. Faculty members serve as consultants and conduct research in their fields, and they are often local, regional, and national opinion leaders. Plus, universities themselves purchase a huge array of products and services, ranging from the mundane (cleaning supplies) to the exotic (scientific instruments).

As noted earlier, you need not be a large company to create mutual wins with a university. Larger companies have more resources and more entry-level openings for graduates, but, as SCG demonstrated, smaller companies can reach out in creative ways to establish personal relationships. Even if you cannot initially draw a large, resource-rich school into your Relationship Web, community colleges and smaller universities would be open to wins.

Fortunately, many of the wins you want from a university—interns from the student population, new hires from graduating classes, consultants from the faculty, additions to the curriculum, or research in a particular area—are automatic wins for the school as well. Serving as a part-time instructor or guest lecturer is a win for your manager and for the school. Other wins you could proactively provide to a university would demand minimal resources. For instance, you can sponsor exhibits or make tickets to campus sporting events and theatrical productions available to other stakeholders and their families. Providing corporate space for art, archeology, and other exhibits requires only coordination by your facilities manager.

The United States is the global center of management education, so most business schools and many undergraduate programs attract students from around the world. Relationships with them can open up international talent pools—well-educated, multilingual foreign nationals who know their countries' customs and cultures and who often have relationships with their nations' business and political elite. As interns, employees, consultants, or translators, these students can provide a window on, and perhaps a door to, foreign markets.

If you doubt the power of synergy among colleges, companies, and communities, consider the concentration of high-technology businesses in the Boston and San Francisco Bay areas. MIT and Stanford University are only two well-known schools in these regions. Scores of other institutions of higher learning constantly refresh and enrich the talent pool, incubate ideas (and businesses), and make these areas among the most attractive places in the nation to live and work.

To apply RAM strategy with colleges and universities, do the following:

- Develop a mix of mutually beneficial activities, rather than only recruiting graduates, only sponsoring exhibits, or only establishing a scholarship.

- Become familiar with the research conducted at the university and with emerging ideas in management, economics, statistical analysis, and technology. Then think broadly about potential wins on both sides.

- Understand that some people criticize relationships between universities and businesses for distorting academic priorities and giving companies wins out of proportion to their investments.

- Learn who on the university's board of trustees or among the active alumni should be in your Relationship Web.

- Buy blocks of tickets to support basketball, baseball, and other sports that don't draw the crowds that football does.

- Listen even more openly than you normally would. Academe differs markedly from business. Also keep a long-term perspective. Your wins might take time to develop as you help a new generation of graduates succeed.

NONPROFIT AND CHARITABLE ORGANIZATIONS: DO WELL BY DOING GOOD

Nonprofit and charitable organizations now have a real awareness of the value of relationships with companies. In the November–December 1996 *Harvard Business Review* article "Profits for Nonprofits: Find a Corporate Partner," Alan R. Andreasen argued that "to survive, nonprofit organizations must develop explicit ties with for-profit corporations" and that "nonprofits must enter into cause-related marketing alliances with corporations." Andreasen noted that nonprofits must begin to "think of themselves not as charities, but as true partners in the marketing effort."

FROM THE RAM PLAYBOOK

At Horizon Bank, as mentioned previously, we've built a win-win relationship with the 100 Black Men of Broward County (which has more than 100 members). The organization lobbied the city of Fort Lauderdale to donate to its first-time home-buyer program land acquired in tax-default cases. Horizon makes construction loans to build houses on that land. The organization keeps deposits at the bank—one of our wins—and gets the flexibility and convenience of preapproved construction loans. After the organization selects the family who is buying the house, the loan can be converted to a mortgage. Then the organization builds the next house on the next parcel of land.

The family wins because the 100 Black Men organization sells the house for the cost of construction (and the city donates the land). The organization wins by bringing home-ownership to people who otherwise might not have achieved it. Horizon wins by fostering racial equality and promoting growth in the area. The bank also wins through improved ratings on fair credit policy toward blacks. More-over, as noted in the Wittenauer case in "Complementors and Competitors: Friends and Foes?" the 100 Black Men organization refers deals to us apart from our role in the home-buyer program.

The evidence of this thinking, on both sides of the relationship, is found in strategic philanthropy. In such philanthropy, companies focus on programs that reflect corporate interests, capabilities, product lines, and locations. Avon supports breast cancer research and treatment. McDonald's funds more than 180 Ronald McDonald houses in more than 14 countries. Kraft Foods contributes to hunger relief and nutrition programs. Home Depot supports Habitat for Humanity.

Properly practiced, strategic philanthropy reflects true commitment to the work of the nonprofit, as well as a "good fit" for the company and its other stakeholders. That fit creates wins for the company as well as for the charity.

To apply RAM in relationships with nonprofit and charitable organizations, follow these tips:

- Be selective—find one, two, or three charities your company and employees can wholeheartedly support. Avoid exhausting your stakeholders with constant solicitations.

- Involve as many employees and senior managers as possible, and extend the effort to other stakeholders whenever you can.

- Pick a nonprofit organization that can use more than money. Opportunities to volunteer will bring employees and managers together.

- In company publications and with awards, recognize employees who do volunteer work and community service not sponsored by the company. Their example will motivate others.

- Support the nonprofit organization when money gets tight, which could mean being conservative when times are good so you have money allocated to the charity when the business cycle turns downward.

THE COMMUNITY: GOOD CORPORATE CITIZENSHIP

The community actually includes all your stakeholders. It also includes people and entities that don't fit into other stakeholder groups—businesses unrelated to yours, civic organizations, social activists, watchdog groups, the man on the street, and constituencies that most managers don't consider until they arise.

A good CRO, if there is one on board, will take a broader view of the community than a director of community relations normally would. The CRO should know the neighborhood and who inhabits nearby commercial and residential buildings. Various groups have different levels of influence in a community, depending on its history and composition. It might be commuters in one town, minority groups in another, or the elderly in another. It's the CRO's job to know how the company's actions might affect the relationship with them.

When management faces a decision, the CRO will consider not only readily identified stakeholders—employees, customers, suppliers, shareholders, environmentalists, and so on—but everyone else as well. In addition to a "stakeholder-impact assessment," a major decision should also be vetted from the legal standpoint (Is there some obscure law against what we're contemplating?), the safety standpoint (What hazards might this decision pose to motorists and pedestrians?), and even the architectural standpoint (Does the design of this facility fit the character and scale of the neighborhood?).

Most communities want the benefits that business brings—jobs, tax revenues, and prestige—but are less enthusiastic about the costs, such as traffic, commercial buildings, and safety hazards. Therefore, it takes focused, sustained effort for a business to truly become a member of the community.

In applying RAM strategy to relations with the community, take these approaches:

- Consider laws and regulations in your planning processes *and* population density, traffic patterns, communications, utilities, infrastructure capabilities, and public- and private-sector services.

- Understand the role of a business in a community as a workplace, economic force, taxpayer, consumer of government services, and institution that people come to depend on in various ways.

- Put a human face on your company by showcasing managers *and* rank-and-file employees in your charitable work, in media relations, and at public hearings.

- Listen to criticism and consider it useful feedback, even if you disagree. But when you arrive at a position that you must defend, defend it well—for the good of other stakeholders and the community.

HAVE EVERYONE ROOTING FOR YOUR SUCCESS

Some companies do a good job with two, three, or, perhaps, four of these constituencies. But hardly any have a strategy for developing all of these relationships into valuable, long-term assets. Instead, they take at least some stakeholders for granted or attend to them only when it's too late.

RAM strategy can preclude the feelings of neglect or injury that often afflict certain stakeholders. (Can't you just hear the head of a charity, university, or city agency saying, "That company has been in town for seven years, and we've never gotten so much as a phone call from them?") But, more important, RAM can enable you to transform all these people from bystanders into stakeholders.

- RAM's applicability to all stakeholders stands among its greatest benefits. In fact, the system must be applied to all stakeholders in order to be a true RAM program.

- Employees and customers represent the core of the relationship asset portfolio. Moreover, satisfied customers are strongly linked to motivated employees.

- Many companies settle for a purely financial connection with their investors and lenders. Both of those stakeholders have more to offer than money alone.

- The media influence all other stakeholders and must therefore be cultivated actively and consistently.

- Competitors and complementors are worth knowing, if only because they represent potential strategic partners of a company.

- Strategic philanthropy aims to build visible, win-win relationships between companies and nonprofit organizations.

- It's easy to leave relationships with universities and the community undeveloped. However, they can be extremely valuable stakeholders provided a company gets to know the people in the universities and the community and the wins that they want and need.

UNCOMMON COMMON SENSE

Having read this far, you may now be a believer in Relationship Asset Management. We certainly hope so. We also hope that you start putting RAM into action immediately. You now have the tools, and you have so much to gain, both personally and professionally.

From time to time as you learned about RAM, it may have struck you as intuitive—basically common sense. Although we've organized these principles into a structured program, much of it really is just common sense. It's common sense to work closely with associates so you can achieve success together. It's common sense to get to know those associates as people, to share your goals with one other, and to help each other reach those goals. Building trust, fixing broken relationships, taking ownership—it's all common sense.

Then why are these things so uncommon? True, some people consistently do some of these things well. Some people are pretty active at networking. Others excel at crafting win-win deals. Many managers focus on customers or employees or other stakeholders, and with good results. Some can put together productive partnerships or attract long-term investors. But very few people use all of these tools and techniques with all of their stakeholders. (As you've seen, we've even dropped the ball a few times.)

It takes a commitment to make any change. We ask you to commit yourself and your organization (that is, the part of it that you oversee), to making the most of every relationship with everyone who comes your way. If you do, you will succeed as you never have before. It worked for us, and it will work for you, too. In the process, you'll come to really enjoy doing business. Instead of the grinding, frustrating, needlessly competitive struggle that doing business without RAM can be, you'll find your life filled with people—many of them true friends—pulling together to make you successful, as you do the same for them.

Once more, here's to a whole new ballgame.

TARGET WINS FOR COMPANY-STAKEHOLDER RELATIONSHIPS

To supplement the material on creating mutual wins in this book, this appendix lists potential target wins for stakeholder groups and for a company working to build relationships with each group. These are offered as wins for each party to shoot for and as catalysts for brainstorming to develop other, more specific wins.

EMPLOYEES

TARGET WINS FOR EMPLOYEES

- Competitive pay and benefits
- An understanding of the business and their role in it, and a sense that management values them in that role
- A sense of motivation, purpose, and teamwork, and a sense of being on a worthwhile collective mission
- Training that will help them understand their jobs within the company and enhance their skills and future employability
- Interesting, fulfilling work in an enjoyable, reduced-friction environment
- Managers and supervisors who give them respect and attention, who care about their safety and welfare, and who solicit their ideas and put the best ones to use

- A manageable, reasonable balance between work and their personal lives
- Working for a respected, and perhaps prestigious, organization

TARGET WINS FOR THE COMPANY

- Lower employee turnover and a staff that stays with the company long enough to understand and care about the business and their jobs
- More productive employees who, because they are committed to the company's goals, strive to deliver high-quality products and services
- Employees who repay the investment in hiring and training
- Independent, self-starting, low-maintenance employees who are aligned with the company's objectives and require less supervision
- Better labor relations because employees who trust management and grasp the basics of the business realize that dividends for investors, low prices for customers, and reinvestment in the company also come out of profits
- Lower absenteeism and fewer instances of tardiness
- Lower rates of inventory "shrinkage" and other forms of theft
- Increased employee loyalty and thus less exposure to employee legal action, sabotage, and theft of intellectual property or accounts
- Better relations throughout the Relationship Web because employees deal with all of the company's stakeholders—and employees themselves are also customers, investors, and community members

CUSTOMERS

TARGET WINS FOR CUSTOMERS

- Superior products and services that meet their needs and deliver value

- Personal attention to individual needs and interests
- Greater ease in doing business as suppliers and merchants come to know their needs and characteristics
- Meaningful recognition for loyalty in the form of discounts or useful premiums
- Appreciation and, if appropriate, rewards for referrals, recommendations, and introductions
- More enjoyable ownership of products and, in business-to-business relationships, smoother and more profitable operations
- Lower "switching costs" due to a reduced need to search out, comparison-shop, and get to know new merchants and suppliers
- Suppliers who will go the extra mile on rush orders, equipment breakdowns, or inventory shortages, and who will do everything possible to assure product availability.

TARGET WINS FOR THE COMPANY
- Lower sales costs due to an improved stream of referrals and reduced "churn" in the customer base
- Improved ability to outmaneuver competitors due to better information on customer needs and closer integration with their processes
- Improved market intelligence from customers willing to share information on their peers and your competitors
- Increased sales on improved market share and greater "share of wallet"
- Higher profits thanks to lower sales costs, higher volume in purchasing, and improved economies of scale in production
- Customers who will understand and work with you during supply shortages, power outages, transportation breakdowns, or other disruptions

- More opportunities to make friends and to help other parties in your Relationship Web

SUPPLIERS

TARGET WINS FOR SUPPLIERS

- Opportunities to proactively develop ways to increase the value they add to their customer relationships, and to share in that increased value
- Reliable customers they can depend on for orders in the long term
- Leads to other potential customers
- References, endorsements, and thank-you letters that help them in their business development efforts
- Advance information about changes that could affect their volume of business with the company
- Flexibility on the part of the buyer
- Improved relations with *their* suppliers

TARGET WINS FOR THE COMPANY

- Cost savings in placing, processing, and handling orders, and a shortened production cycle
- Shorter product-development cycles (and better products)
- Willingness of the supplier to go the extra mile during shortages or when otherwise necessary
- Fair warning about price increases, late deliveries, or other factors that could affect business

INVESTORS

TARGET WINS FOR INVESTORS

- Returns commensurate with the risk of the investment
- Peace of mind in knowing that the investment is as secure as management can make it

- Reliable information on the company's plans, performance, and prospects, which enables the investor to decide if he should be a stakeholder in the company
- Lower investment costs, which include research expense, brokers' fees, taxes, and other transaction fees
- Pride of ownership in an ethical, well-managed company that treats all its stakeholders fairly
- Minimal risk of lawsuits, regulatory action, and other problems arising from managerial malfeasance, all of which damage the stock price
- Enough confidence in the company that a decrease in the stock price due to stock market conditions or the business cycle represents a buying opportunity

TARGET WINS FOR THE COMPANY

- Long-term investors who understand the company and trust management, and thus reduced stock-price volatility
- Continued access to equity in the public markets or from private sources
- Fair treatment from analysts who have come to believe, and perhaps believe *in,* the management team
- Trouble avoided by operating and reporting within generally accepted accounting principles, SEC regulations, and the law
- Boosters and allies who speak well of the company and participate in the company's success, and perhaps contribute through their resources and connections
- Improved relations with investors who play other stakeholder roles, including employees, retirees, strategic allies, community members, and charitable trusts

BOARDS OF DIRECTORS

TARGET WINS FOR BOARD MEMBERS

- Closer contact with a wider range of stakeholders and, therefore, better information on each constituency

- Smoother, more effective corporate governance and more productive board meetings
- Reduced risk of being blindsided by a representative of a stakeholder group
- Compensation in the form of stock in the company
- Extended contacts and a broader Relationship Web for each director
- More intimate knowledge of the company and greater confidence that management is attending to the interests of all stakeholders
- Prestige of being on the board of a successful and respected company

TARGET WINS FOR THE COMPANY

- Improved guidance from the board of directors
- Increased access to the Relationship Web of each board member
- Reduced risks similar to those realized by the board itself
- Increased ability to attract competent, committed board members

STRATEGIC ALLIES

TARGET WINS FOR BOTH PARTIES IN AN ALLIANCE

- Revenue and profits that would otherwise be forgone
- Access to markets, technologies, processes, or talent that they now lack
- Lower financial risk compared with purchasing or building the capabilities accessed by means of the alliance
- Faster product development, production cycle, or time to market
- Improved competitive position
- Protection of current markets or ability to penetrate new markets, or both

- Heightened ability to work as a team to produce solutions to customer and operational problems

- Enhanced reputation in the eyes of customers, the media, and other stakeholders

- Easier and less costly access to foreign markets (in alliances with overseas partners)

BANKS AND OTHER LENDERS

TARGET WINS FOR BANKS AND OTHER LENDERS

- A steady source of deposits and a growing user of the bank's services

- A commercial customer who keeps them informed, is easy to do business with, and understands the pressures they face

- A growing account that reflects well on their skills as a business developer

- A source of referrals to new commercial and personal accounts

TARGET WINS FOR THE COMPANY

- More attention, better service, and faster resolution of errors

- Faster approval of loans and perhaps a larger loan or better interest rate

- Good references and a solid "bank story" when other creditors or potential lenders call your bank for them

- Personal guidance regarding financial products, including the ones to avoid

- News of deals, developments, and people you should know because most bankers are well-wired into the business and civic networks in their communities and regions

MEDIA

TARGET WINS FOR THE MEDIA OUTLET

- Good leads to fresh and interesting stories and story ideas
- Reliable contacts in the business community who can provide good quotes, fast responses to questions, and referrals to other experts
- Opportunities to deal with businesspeople who will go beyond the usual "company spokesperson" patter to explain the whole story or offer a new perspective
- Assistance (at smaller publications and broadcast outlets) in the form of graphics, diagrams, photos, video footage, or audio tapes
- Contacts who take an active interest in the journalist's work, who write thank-you notes, and who make them look good to their bosses
- Material that enhances and perhaps showcases advertisers, and perhaps the purchase of advertising itself

TARGET WINS FOR THE COMPANY

- Increased credibility among other stakeholders, particularly customers, prospects, and current and potential employees and investors
- Name recognition that attracts new stakeholders and facilitates contact
- Print pieces that you can use in advertising and direct-mail campaigns or in making a "touch"
- Becoming a recognized source so journalists come to you for quotes, confirmation, and contacts, which makes PR almost effortless
- People in the media who will be willing to help you get your story out, or at least listen to your side with an open mind, in the event of a management error, product liability situation, or other crisis

- Contacts who will give you a heads-up on future stories that could affect your business

COMPLEMENTORS AND COMPETITORS

TARGET WINS FOR COMPLEMENTORS AND COMPETITORS (ON BOTH SIDES)

- Improved information on the marketplace and industry developments
- Fewer resource-draining and potentially damaging price or market share "wars"
- Greater opportunities in an expanding market
- Economies of scale and other savings achieved by pooling resources (as in the real-estate industry's MLS system)
- Reduced risk of legal action and antitrust suits brought by offended companies in the same industry
- Greater industry solidarity against external threats, such as unreasonably restrictive government regulation
- Positive media coverage
- Established "rules of engagement" rather than bruising or destructive competition

COLLEGES AND UNIVERSITIES

TARGET WINS FOR COLLEGES AND UNIVERSITIES

- Courses and internships that prepare students for careers in business (or, depending on the company, technology, design, architecture, engineering, and other fields)
- Employment opportunities for students and graduates and, at times, faculty members on sabbatical or in consulting roles

- Support from an influential and affluent segment of the community, and a higher profile in the region
- Contributions from alumni who remain in the area to work, as well as assistance in raising funds
- Support for university research centers and for research by individual professors
- Shared knowledge from the company on the markets and economy, workplace developments, and new methods and technologies

TARGET WINS FOR THE COMPANY

- Lower recruiting costs for new hires and higher-quality hires
- Reasonably priced, motivated, intelligent part-time workers and interns
- Access to new technologies, methods, ideas, and developments
- Enhanced ability to "think young" and understand young adults
- Exposure to cutting-edge ideas and developments
- Tax write-offs for donations and donated equipment
- Support from an influential and highly regarded segment of the community
- Opportunities for management to expand into new areas due to exposure to foreign students, off-beat courses, and new ideas
- Satisfaction of cultivating the fruits of higher education: discoveries that better people's lives, reduced poverty, a skilled workforce, and enrichment from the arts and the pursuit of knowledge
- Satisfaction and engagement of employees, who are also proud of their connection with the institution of learning

NONPROFIT AND CHARITABLE ORGANIZATIONS

TARGET WINS FOR THE NONPROFIT ORGANIZATION

- Donations of money, goods, and equipment, and perhaps other corporate resources such as office space or space for events
- Contributions of time and talent from the company's employees
- Continuity of funding (provided that the donor is committed and plans properly)
- Enhanced ability to attract media coverage, particularly in joint efforts with the company
- Credibility with other corporate donors and potential donors
- Improved ability to recruit and pay staff, and to plan for the future

TARGET WINS FOR THE COMPANY

- Higher standing in the community and among other stakeholders thanks to the image—and reality—of good corporate citizenship
- Improved ability to attract employees and investors
- Increased customer loyalty of the type enjoyed by Newman's Own, Ben & Jerry's Ice Cream, and The Body Shop
- Increased esprit de corps among managers and employees who know one another better through shared off-the-job experiences
- Enhanced ability to attract positive media coverage
- Goodwill that can counter company faults and failures (Even people who cannot abide Jerry Lewis or the "Jerry's

kids" theme allow that he has done a world of good for children with muscular dystrophy.)

- Satisfaction in knowing that, as a company, you and your employees are sharing your good fortune and are giving back to the community

GOVERNMENT AGENCIES

TARGET WINS FOR THE GOVERNMENT

- Smoother operations when they deal with your business because you understand the need for regulations and consistently comply with them
- Campaign contributions for elected officials and financial support for other government workers as appropriate—for instance, contributions to the Policemen's Benevolent Association or the Firemen's Fund
- Valuable contacts in the private sector
- Opportunities to look good in the eyes of their bosses

TARGET WINS FOR THE COMPANY

- Decreased risk of unwarranted government involvement in your business
- Improved representation of your case in proceedings such as zoning hearings, tax assessment appeals, and legislative initiatives
- Smoother interfaces with government agencies and workers because they occur in the context of a relationship
- Improved contacts beyond the government (People in the city, state, and federal government—particularly elected officials—typically have large, powerful networks.)
- Earlier information on regulatory or legislative changes because you follow these events more closely or because your contacts warn you, and thus improved ability to respond

COMMUNITY

TARGET WINS FOR THE COMMUNITY

- Good jobs that attract residents to the area and enable them to be productive and to support other businesses and institutions
- Economic strength and growth
- Steadily increasing tax revenues
- Clean air and water, and reasonable demands on transportation, utilities, and other infrastructure
- Synergy with the aims of other community members, such as schools, churches, charities, and law enforcement
- Positive "vibes" and a good reputation due to the business base, as in Austin (high-tech), Nashville (music), and Vancouver (filmmaking), or to a single company, as in Redmond (Microsoft)

TARGET WINS FOR THE COMPANY

- Pride in the organization on the part of employees and all other stakeholder groups
- Greater trust and friendliness, rather than suspicion and hostility, with each passing year
- Reduced risk of protests, actions at law, sabotage, and disruption of operations
- General approval from the population, which gives government officials and other stakeholders, such as hospitals and utilities, the latitude to go the extra mile when the company needs it
- Potential tax breaks, if they're needed for survival or to make an expansion effort economically feasible
- Easier relocation of new employees and their families to an attractive area where they will quickly feel at home

INDEX

A

adversity, sharing with stakeholders, 111
alliances, target wins, 239
Anderson, Ken, 2
Andreasen, Alan R., 226
appropriateness, stakeholders,
107
asking questions, 88-91

B

banks
    relationships with, 218-219
    target wins, 240
Bertrand, John, 116
betrayal in relationships, 146
board members, target wins,
238
bonding in relationships, 102,
109
Bonington, Chris, 168
boundaries in relationships,
108
    breaching, 144
businesses, killing, 189-193
Byne, John A., 189

C

calls, contacts, 73-75
Carroll, Bob, 24
*Chainsaw: The Notorious
Career of Al Dunlap in the
Era of Profit-at-Any-Price,* 189
charities
    relationships with, 31-32,
    226-228
    target wins, 244
chief relationship officers.
    See CROs
civility in relationships, 146
cold calls, contacts, 73-75
colleges
    relationships with, 224-226
    target wins, 242
commitments, keeping, 120
communication, maintaining,
183
communities, target wins, 246
companies
    killing, 189-193
    target wins, 235-243
competitors
    relationships with, 7,
    222-223
    target wins, 242

complementors
    relationships with, 222-223
    target wins, 242
confidences, respecting, 122
connections, contacts, 75-78
constructive criticism, 121
contacts
    cold calls, 73-75
    connections, 75-78
    cultivating, 3-8, 64-67
    making, 72-73
    warm calls, 73-75
contracts, RAM, 179
corporate citizenship, 229-230
cost-benefit analysis, 170
    relationships, 39-40
credit, sharing, 121
criticism, constructive, 121
CROs (chief relationship officers), 18-19, 43-50, 55-59
    hiring, 50
    model, 55-56
    responsibilities, 59
    roles, 53
    support for, 58
Curtis, Richard, 142
customers
    courting, 92-93
    relationships with, 211-212
    target wins, 235

D

Delsohn, Steve, 188
demands in relationships, 29-31
Dunlap, Al, 189

E

educational institutions, relationships with, 224-226
Eisenhower, Dwight D., 142
empathy in relationships, 113
employees
    relationships with, 209-210
    target wins, 234
expectations (false) in relationships, 136
exploitation in relationships, 38

F

false expectations in relationships, 136
Firestone, Harvey, 128
flexible rosters, creating, 203-204
flowcharts, RAM, creating, 186
focus in relationships, 135
Ford, Henry, 128
friendship, 121

G

gap analysis, 170
   in relationships, 39-40
Gates, Bill, 6
government
   agencies, target wins, 245
   courting, 95

H

Hardaway, Tim, 96, 220
Hatch, Orrin, 6
helping stakeholders, 111
high switching costs, RAM,
  180
hiring, CROs, 50
How to Work for a Jerk and
*Work Would Be Great If It
Weren't for the People,* 143
hygiene, importance of, 141

I

implicit wins, 151
information, sharing with
  stakeholders, 111
investing in relationships,
  198-199
investors
   relationships with, 215-216
   target wins, 237

invitations, stakeholders, 110
issues, resolving, 184

J–K–L

Johnson, Earvin "Magic," 81

lenders
   relationships with, 218-219
   target wins, 240

M

maintaining relationships, 139
media
   relationships with, 220-221
   outlets, target wins, 241
*Men at Work: The Craft of
Baseball,* 62
Microsoft, relationship failures,
  5
Miller, Paul, 145
multiple-link insurance, RAM,
  178

N

Netscape Communications,
  Microsoft relationship, 6
networks in relationships, 8-12
   identifying, 37-38
   spoking out, 85-88

nonmonetary winning, 83-84
nonprofit organizations
   relationships with, 226-228
   target wins, 244

O

overtrusting, 123
ownership in relationships, 43-59, 138
   assigning, 17
   CROs, 43-59

P

Palmer, Pete, 24
Parker, Dorothy, 122
personality problems in relationships, 142
plans, adjusting, 184
Pomarico, Frank, 188
poor hygiene in relationships, 141
prejudicial attitudes in relationships, 145
preparation in relationships, 134
prioritization, RAM, 199-203
prioritizing, stakeholders, 12
proactive wins, providing, 122

problems in relationships
   finding, 150-157
   fixing, 149-168
   resolving, 184
processes, trusting, 126

Q–R

questions, asking, 88-91

RAM (Relationship Asset Management), 14-15
   assessments, 174-176
   cost-benefit analysis, 170
   CROs, hiring, 50
   developing, 16-17, 35-37
   exploitation, 38
   flowcharts, creating, 186
   gap analysis, 170
   goals, 36
   insurance, 177-181
   maintaining, 182
   other strategies relating to, 40
   planning, 176
   prioritization, 199-203
   proposing, 170
   risks, 36
   starting, 169

success factors, 36

systems, developing, 185

U.S. business culture, 192-193

relations

   organizational information, 68-69

   personal information, 69-72

Relationship Asset Management. *See* RAM

relationships

   alliances, target wins, 239

   banks, target wins, 240

   betrayal, 146

   board members, target wins, 238

   boundaries, breaching, 144

   building

      organizational information, 68-69

      personal information, 69-72

   charities, 31-32

      target wins, 244

   civility, 146

   colleges and universities, target wins, 242

   communities, target wins, 246

   companies, target wins, 235-243

competitors, 7

   target wins, 242

complementors, target wins, 242

contacts

   connections, 75-78

   cold calls, 73-75

   making, 72-73

   warm calls, 73-75

cost-benefit analysis, 39-40

CROs (chief relationship officers), 18-19

cultivating, 3-8, 26-28

customers

   courting, 92-93

   target wins, 235

demands, 29-31

employees, target wins, 234

false expectations, 136

flexible rosters, creating, 203-204

focus, 135

gap analysis, 39-40

government

   agencies, target wins, 245

   courting, 95

investing in, 198-199

investors, target wins, 237

killers

   Type I, 133-141

   Type II, 141-146

lenders, target wins, 240

long-term value, understanding, 194

maintaining, 139, 204-205

media outlets, target wins, 241

ownership, 43-59, 138
  assigning, 17
  CROs, 43-59

personality problems, 142

poor hygiene, 141

prejudicial attitudes, 145

preparation, 134

problems, fixing, 149-168

RAM (Relationship Asset Management), 14-15
  assessments, 174-176
  cost-benefit analysis, 170
  developing, 16-17, 35-37
  exploitation, 38
  gap analysis, 170
  goals, 36
  insurance, 177-181
  maintaining, 182
  other strategies relating to, 40
  planning, 176
  prioritization, 199-203
  proposing, 170
  risks, 36
  starting, 169
  success factors, 36
  systems, 185

returns, 196

social shortcomings, 141

stakeholders
  adversity sharing, 111
  appropriateness, 107
  banks, 218-219
  bonding with, 102, 109
  boundaries, 108
  charities, 226-228
  colleges, 224-226
  competitors, 222-223
  complementors, 222-223
  coping with, 113
  customers, 211-212
  empathy, 113
  employees, 209-210
  helping, 111
  information, sharing, 111
  investors, 215-216
  invitations, 110
  media, 220-221
  nonprofit organizations, 226-228
  perceptions, 114
  stages, 103
  strategic allies, 217
  suppliers, 213-214
  time spent with, 104
  universities, 224-225

suppliers, target wins, 237

supply, ensuring, 33-35

trust, 118
  earning, 119
vendors, courting, 94
web, 8-12
  identifying, 37-38
  spoking out, 85-88
  win-win zones, moving to, 21-23
  wins, defining, 19-20
reputations, trustworthiness, establishing, 123
Richardson, Tom, 96
Riley, Pat, 80
Robbie, Joe, 148
Robinson, Patrick, 116
Rocker, John, 132
rosters, flexible, creating, 203-204

S

Sahadi, Lou, 148
schedules (touch schedules), 183
Schultz, Jim, 132
Smith, Robert, 208
social shortcomings in relationships, 141
spoking out, relationship webs, 85-88
stages of relationships, 103
stakeholders, 209
  adversity, sharing, 111
  alliances, target wins, 239

appropriateness, 107
banks, 218-219
  target wins, 240
board members, target wins, 238
bonds, building, 102, 109
boundaries, 108
charities, 226-228
  target wins, 244
colleges, 224-226
  target wins, 242
communities, target wins, 246
companies, target wins, 235-243
competitors, 222-223
  target wins, 242
complementors, 222-223
  target wins, 242
coping with, 113
customers, 211-212
  target wins, 235
empathy in relationships, 113
employees, 209-210
  target wins, 234
flexible rosters, creating, 203-204
government agencies, target wins, 245
inclusion, 180
information, sharing, 111
investing in, 198-199

investors, 215-216

  target wins, 237

invitations, 110

knowing, stages, 103

lenders, target wins, 240

maintaining, 204-205

media, 220-221

  outlets, target wins, 241

nonprofit organizations, 226-228

people, viewing as, 114

problems, fixing, 164-165

questions, asking, 90

relationship webs, 9, 12

strategic allies, 217

suppliers, 213-214

  target wins, 237

time spent with, frequency, 104

trust, value of, 128

universities, 224-225

stakeholders, helping, 111

strategic allies in relationships, 217

suppliers

  relationships, 213-214

  target wins, 237

supply, ensuring in relationships, 33-35

systems, RAM, developing, 185

T

target wins

  alliances, 239

  banks, 240

  board members, 238

  charities, 244

  colleges and universities, 242

  communities, 246

  companies, 235-243

  competitors, 242

  complementors, 242

  customers, 235

  employees, 234

  government agencies, 245

  investors, 237

  lenders, 240

  media outlets, 241

  suppliers, 237

teams, building trust, 130

Thorn, John, 24

touch schedules, 183

trust in relationships, 118

  commitments, keeping, 120

  confidences, respecting, 122

  credit, sharing, 121

  criticism, constructive, 121

  earning, 119

  friendship, 121

  overtrusting, 123

proactive wins, providing, 122

processes, 126

reputation, establishing, 123

stakeholders, value of, 128

teams, building, 130

tone, 122

truth, telling, 120

Turco, Mary, 100

Type I relationship killers, 133-141

Type II relationship killers, 141-146

U–V

universities
relationships with, 224-226
target wins, 242

vendors, courting, 94

W–X–Y–Z

Waldron, Bob (vice president of General Mills), 84

warm calls, contacts, 73-75

webs, relationships, 8-12
identifying, 37-38
spoking out, 85-88

Will, George F., 62

win-win zones in relationships, moving to, 21-23

wins
asking for, 88
delivering, 184
designing, 184
finding ways to get, 82
implicit wins, 151
looking for, 97
nonmonetary, 82-84
proactive, providing, 122
relationships, defining, 19-20
spoking out, 85-88
target
alliances, 239
banks, 240
board members, 238
charities, 244
colleges and universities, 242
communities, 246
companies, 235-243
competitors, 242
complementors, 242
customers, 235
employees, 234
government agencies, 245
investors, 237
lenders, 240
media outlets, 241
suppliers, 237
written agreements, RAM, 179